# CREATIONISM IN TWENTIETH-CENTURY AMERICA

Volume 4

# THE ANTIEVOLUTION PAMPHLETS OF WILLIAM BELL RILEY

# THE ANTIEVOLUTION PAMPHLETS OF WILLIAM BELL RILEY

Edited by
WILLIAM VANCE TROLLINGER

LONDON AND NEW YORK

First published in 1995 by Garland Publishing, Inc.

This edition first published in 2022
by Routledge
2 Park Square, Milton Park, Abingdon, Oxon OX14 4RN

and by Routledge
605 Third Avenue, New York, NY 10158

*Routledge is an imprint of the Taylor & Francis Group, an informa business*

© 1995 Series Introduction Ronald L. Numbers © 1995 Introduction copyright William Vance Trollinger, Jr.

All rights reserved. No part of this book may be reprinted or reproduced or utilised in any form or by any electronic, mechanical, or other means, now known or hereafter invented, including photocopying and recording, or in any information storage or retrieval system, without permission in writing from the publishers.

*Trademark notice*: Product or corporate names may be trademarks or registered trademarks, and are used only for identification and explanation without intent to infringe.

*British Library Cataloguing in Publication Data*
A catalogue record for this book is available from the British Library

ISBN: 978-0-367-43553-0 (Set)
ISBN: 978-1-00-314991-0 (Set) (ebk)
ISBN: 978-0-367-41505-1 (Volume 4) (hbk)
ISBN: 978-0-367-41508-2 (Volume 4) (pbk)
ISBN: 978-0-367-81491-5 (Volume 4) (ebk)

DOI: 10.4324/9780367814915

**Publisher's Note**
The publisher has gone to great lengths to ensure the quality of this reprint but points out that some imperfections in the original copies may be apparent.

**Disclaimer**
The publisher has made every effort to trace copyright holders and would welcome correspondence from those they have been unable to trace.

# New Preface to the Re-issue of 2021

This anthology of primary documents related to the early history of creationism in the United States first appeared a quarter century ago, in 1995. My interest in the topic had been aroused by my years of research on creationism, which resulted in *The Creationists* (New York: Alfred A. Knopf, 1992). In the meantime, a former student of mine, Edward J. Larson, had published an excellent legal survey, *Trial and Error: The American Controversy over Creation and Evolution* (New York: Oxford University Press, 1985). The philosopher of science Michael Ruse had published the edited volume *But Is It Science? The Philosophical Question in the Creation/Evolution Controversy* (Amherst, NY: Prometheus Books, 1988); and the anthropologist Christopher P. Toumey had just released *God's Own Scientists: Creationists in a Secular World* (New Brunswick, NJ: Rutgers University Press, 1994). Led by Willard B. Gatewood's *Preachers Pedagogues and Politicians: The Evolution Controversy in North Carolina, 1920–1927* (Chapel Hill: University of North Carolina Press, 1966), local studies had also begun to appear. Nevertheless, few, if any, research libraries had begun collecting creationist literature; and not one, to my knowledge, possessed even a complete run of the *Creation Research Society Quarterly*, launched in 1964.

During the past quarter century the landscape of creationism has changed dramatically. Since 1995 the institutional heart of creationism has shifted from the Institute for Creation Research, founded by Henry M. Morris in southern California in 1972, to Ken Ham's Answers in Genesis, headquartered in northern Kentucky. In 2007 the charismatic Australian-born Ham opened a $27-million Creation Museum in Petersburg, Kentucky, across the Ohio River from Cincinnati. Forty-five miles away, in Williamstown, Kentucky, Ham in July 2016 opened an Ark Encounter featuring a "life-size" replica of Noah's ark, at a projected cost of $150 million.

Such growth has attracted considerable attention, such as Susan L. Trollinger and William Vance Trollinger Jr., *Righting America at the Creation Museum* (Baltimore: Johns Hopkins University Press, 2016), and James S. Bielo, *Ark Encounter: The Making of a Creationist Theme Park* (New York: New York University Press, 2018).

The literature on the general history of creationism in the twentieth century has exploded, symbolized most dramatically by Edward J. Larson's Pulitzer Prize-winning volume *Summer for the Gods: The Scopes Trial and America's Continuing Debate over Science and Religion* (New York: Basic Books, 1997). Other significant contributions include Michael Lienesch, *In the Beginning: Fundamentalism, the Scopes Trial, and the Making of the Antievolution Movement* (Chapel Hill: University of North Carolina, 2007); Adam Laats, *Fundamentalism and Education in the Scopes Era: God, Darwin, and the Roots of America's Culture Wars* (New York: Palgrave Macmillan, 2010); Jeffrey P. Moran, *American Genesis: The Evolution Controversies from Scopes to Creation Science* (New York: Oxford University Press, 2012); and Adam R. Shapiro, *Trying Biology: The Scopes Trial, Textbooks, and the Antievolution Movement in American Schools* (Chicago: University of Chicago Press, 2013).

Still, access to creationist sources before the early 1960s remains patchy. To help remedy this condition, Routledge has agreed to reissue the 10-volume set of *Creationism in Twentieth-Century America*. I thank them for their continuing interest.

Ronald L. Numbers
April 2021

# CREATIONISM IN TWENTIETH-CENTURY AMERICA

*A Ten-Volume Anthology of Documents, 1903–1961*

Series Editor

**RONALD L. NUMBERS**
*University of Wisconsin–Madison*
*William Coleman Professor of the*
*History of Science and Medicine*

A GARLAND SERIES

# Series Contents

1. ANTIEVOLUTION BEFORE WORLD WAR I

2. CREATION-EVOLUTION DEBATES

3. THE ANTIEVOLUTION WORKS OF ARTHUR I. BROWN

4. THE ANTIEVOLUTION PAMPHLETS OF WILLIAM BELL RILEY

5. THE CREATIONIST WRITINGS OF BYRON C. NELSON

6. THE ANTIEVOLUTION PAMPHLETS OF HARRY RIMMER

7. SELECTED WORKS OF GEORGE McCREADY PRICE

8. THE EARLY WRITINGS OF HAROLD W. CLARK AND FRANK LEWIS MARSH

9. EARLY CREATIONIST JOURNALS

10. CREATION AND EVOLUTION IN THE EARLY AMERICAN SCIENTIFIC AFFILIATION

*VOLUME*

# 4

# THE ANTIEVOLUTION PAMPHLETS OF WILLIAM BELL RILEY

Edited with an introduction by
WILLIAM VANCE TROLLINGER, JR.
*Messiah College*

GARLAND PUBLISHING, Inc.
New York & London
1995

Series introduction copyright © 1995 Ronald L. Numbers
Introduction copyright © 1995 William Vance Trollinger, Jr.
All rights reserved

**Library of Congress Cataloging-in-Publication Data**

Riley, W. B. (William Bell), 1861–1947.
    The antievolution pamphlets of William Bell Riley / edited with an introduction by William Vance Trollinger, Jr.
       p.   cm. — (Creationism in twentieth-century America ; v. 4)
    Includes bibliographical references.
    ISBN 0-8153-1805-7 (alk. paper)
    1. Creationism—United States.  2. Fundamentalism—United States.  3. Dispensationalism.  I. Trollinger, William Vance. II. Title.  III. Series.
BS651.R546  1995
231.7'65—dc20                                                  94-43258
                                                                             CIP

Printed on acid-free, 250-year-life paper
Manufactured in the United States of America

# Contents

| | |
|---|---|
| Series Introduction | vii |
| Volume Introduction | ix |
| *Are the Scriptures Scientific?* | 1 |
| *Darwinism; or, Is Man a Developed Monkey?* | 33 |
| *Darwin's Philosophy and the Flood* | 57 |
| *Evolution—A False Philosophy* | 87 |
| *The Scientific Accuracy of the Sacred Scriptures* | 119 |
| *The Theory of Evolution Tested by Mathematics* | 139 |
| *The Theory of Evolution—Does It Tend to Atheism?* | 171 |
| *The Theory of Evolution—Does It Tend To Anarchy?* | 191 |
| *Hitlerism; or, The Philosophy of Evolution in Action* | 207 |
| Acknowledgments | 221 |

# Series Introduction

In recent years creationism has enjoyed a stunning renaissance both in the United States and around the world. Public opinion polls show that 47 percent of Americans, including one quarter of college graduates, believe that "God created man pretty much in his present form at one time within the last 10,000 years." In the early 1980s two states, Arkansas and Louisiana, passed laws mandating the teaching of "creation science" whenever "evolution science" was taught in the public schools. The United States Supreme Court subsequently overturned these laws, but creationists actively—and often successfully—continue to promote their cause in local schools and churches.

Since the early 1960s creationism has become increasingly identified with a particular nonevolutionary belief known as "scientific creationism" or "creation science." Scientific creationists believe that all life on earth originated no more than 10,000 years ago, and some argue that the entire universe is equally young. To explain the appearance of age suggested by the fossil record, they typically invoke Noah's flood, which, they claim, deposited virtually the entire geological column in the span of a year or so.

Before the 1960s relatively few Americans, including religious fundamentalists, subscribed to such restrictive views of earth history. At the height of the antievolution controversies of the 1920s, for example, most creationists who expressed themselves on the subject embraced interpretations of the book of Genesis that allowed them to accept the evidence of historical geology for the antiquity of life on earth. They generally did so in one of two ways: either by assuming that the "days" of Genesis 1 really meant "ages" or by interposing a gap of perhaps hundreds of millions of years between the creation "in the beginning" and the relatively recent Edenic creation (or restoration, as some would call it) associated with Adam and Eve. Only a few fundamentalists at the time, mostly Seventh-day Adventists, insisted on the recent appearance of life and on the geological significance of the deluge. In recent years, however, through the influence of books such as John C. Whitcomb, Jr. and Henry M. Morris's *The Genesis Flood* (1961), organizations such as the Creation Research Society (1963) and institutions such as the Institute for Creation Research (1972), the so-called flood geologists, now known as scientific creationists, have co-opted the very name creationist for their once peculiar views.

Despite the undeniable importance of antievolutionism in American cultural history, few libraries, academic or otherwise, have collected more than the odd book or pamphlet on creationism, and early creationist periodicals are almost impossible to find. Whether the result of prejudice or indifference, such neglect has made it difficult for students and scholars to explore the development of creationist thought in the twentieth century. This collection of reprinted documents from the first six decades of the century makes available some of the most widely read works on creationism by such stalwarts as Arthur I. Brown, William Bell Riley, Harry Rimmer, Byron C. Nelson, George McCready Price, Harold W. Clark, and Frank Lewis Marsh. It also reprints, for the first time, three of the earliest and rarest creationist journals in America: the *Creationist*, the *Bulletin of Deluge Geology*, and the *Forum for the Correlation of Science and the Bible*.

# INTRODUCTION

It is difficult to overstate William Bell Riley's importance to the early fundamentalist movement; it is well-nigh impossible to exaggerate his prodigious energy. In the years between the world wars, when he was in his 60s and 70s and pastor of a church with thousands of members, Riley founded and directed the first interdenominational organization of fundamentalists, served as an active leader of the fundamentalist faction in the Northern Baptist Convention, edited a variety of fundamentalist periodicals, wrote innumerable books and articles and pamphlets (including, in the less-polemical vein, a forty-volume exposition of the entire Bible), presided over a fundamentalist Bible school and its expanding network of churches, and masterminded a fundamentalist takeover of the Minnesota Baptist Convention. Besides all this, in these years William Bell Riley also established himself as one of the leading antievolutionists in America.

This volume consists of nine antievolution pamphlets that Riley wrote and published in the interwar years. The introduction provides a brief synopsis of Riley's antievolutionist ideas and activities, with some effort to place this work in the larger context of Riley's career, and includes discussion of these pamphlets.[1]

William Bell Riley was born on March 22, 1861, in Green County, Indiana. The Civil War broke out soon thereafter, and his father, a native Southerner, moved the family across the Ohio into Kentucky. At an early age Riley was put to work on the family tobacco farm, but the ambitious and bright young man had no intention of spending his life plowing the fields. Enthralled with the trials he witnessed in the county courthouse, Riley originally planned to become an attorney. But at the age of twenty, Riley, whose parents were devout evangelicals, surrendered to a "divine call" to become a preacher.

Riley scraped together the funds to attend Hanover College, a small Presbyterian school in Indiana. Graduating in 1885 (ranking first in debate, it should be noted), he immediately went on to Southern Baptist Seminary in Louisville, where the conservative theology of his childhood was reinforced. After graduation in 1888 Riley served as a pastor in Lafayette, Indiana, followed by a ministerial stint in Bloomington, Illinois. Then, in 1893, Riley accepted the pastorate of Calvary Baptist Church in Chicago. Riley had dreamed of creating a great urban church; now he had the chance. He seemed to be succeeding, as membership increased rapidly. Riley soon came to the conclusion, however, that he could have more impact in a city that was not quite so large. Hence, in 1897 he accepted the pastorate of the First Baptist Church of Minneapolis.

Riley immediately began shaping his new church into a center of evangelism. Sunday morning services always ended with an altar call, and Sunday evening and weekday services were revivalistic in nature. The tall, handsome preacher with a magnetic personality and powerful voice enjoyed remarkable success: within one year membership had jumped from 585 to 855. Over the next decade the church continued to grow rapidly; by 1942, when Riley retired from the pulpit, First Baptist Church had 3,550 members.

Whether at First Baptist or out on one of his revival swings through the Midwest, Riley preached a theologically conservative message, including an emphasis on the deity of Christ, Christ's vicarious atonement and bodily resurrection, the sinfulness of human beings, and their justification by faith. Two types of doctrines were of particular importance, doctrines that had become popular in evangelical circles in the late nineteenth century and would come to serve as the pillars of fundamentalist theology. First was the notion of biblical inerrancy: Riley asserted that the Bible was verbally inspired of God, and hence literally accurate, without error. Second, and connected to the first, was Riley's belief in the personal, premillennial, and imminent return of Jesus Christ. Riley was committed to dispensationalism, a form of premillennialism that holds that: history is segmented into dispensations; read literally, biblical prophecies are a certain guide to the past, present, and future of human experience; and, Christ's kingdom belongs solely to a future age, with the present age marked by widespread decadence in society and apostasy in the church.

The young minister could see apostasy (as well as decadence) sprouting up all around him. Riley was horrified that so-called Christians were championing a liberal or modernist theology that took a sociohistorical view of the Bible, denying its divine inspiration and bringing into question the veracity of the biblical accounts of miracles and other supernatural events (including the Virgin Birth and bodily resurrection of Christ). Not one to keep quiet, in 1909 the agitated minister and evangelist went on the attack with the publication of a book entitled *The Finality of the*

*Higher Criticism; or, The Theory of Evolution and False Theology.* As the title makes quite clear, Riley was convinced that this "false theology" was the natural outgrowth of an acceptance of evolutionary philosophy; to put it another way, from the beginning, antievolution was central to Riley's antimodernism. Two chapters in *Finality* dealt directly with evolutionism; they were later reprinted separately as pamphlets, with different titles and very minor revisions, and are included in this collection: *The Scientific Accuracy of the Sacred Scriptures* (1920) and *Darwinism; or, Is Man a Developed Monkey?* (1929).

In the preface to *Finality* Riley proposed that conservatives unite to fight the liberals and their theology. At the time Riley's call went unheeded. But then came World War I. Americans were thrown into a state of cultural alarm, as they worried that "German barbarism" would swamp American civilization. Conservative evangelicals, caught up in this cultural anxiety, became much more receptive to attacks on modernist theology and evolutionary philosophy, particularly given that such ideas had become associated with German thought. Riley himself became increasingly strident in the war years; his 1917 book, *The Menace of Modernism*, is much more alarmist than *Finality of Higher Criticism*, particularly as regards the author's conviction that liberal theology and Darwinism had captured higher education in America, including many church-related colleges.

By the end of the war years Riley, through his publications and through his work in organizing and addressing prophecy conferences (which World War I made quite popular), had established himself as a minor religious figure on the national scene. At war's end he moved to center stage. Determined to take advantage of the growing anxieties among conservative evangelicals, Riley organized a World Conference on the Fundamentals of the Faith, which was held May 25–June 1, 1919, in Philadelphia. Over 6,000 people attended. Riley delivered the keynote address, in which he proclaimed that this meeting was "an event of more historic moment than the nailing up, at Wittenberg, of Martin Luther's ninety-five Theses."[2]

As Riley saw it, what made this gathering historic was that it marked the creation of an interdenominational organization, the World's Christian Fundamentals Association (WCFA), which would actively promote the "true gospel" and aggressively combat the advances of modernism. As its initial goal, the WCFA, with Riley as president, sought the elimination of modernist theology from Protestant denominations. Toward that end, the organization began with a bang: a well-publicized national tour and the establishment of committees that were charged with developing lists of WCFA-recommended ("Bible-believing") colleges, seminaries, and missions organizations.

It soon become clear, however, that the WCFA would not be able to eliminate modernism from the established denominations. As an outside organization there were limits to what the WCFA could do to force changes, and Riley and company steadfastly refused to establish the WCFA as an alternative denomination. Hence, by 1922 or so the WCFA began to place less emphasis on cleansing the major denominations; this task would be left to antimodernist efforts from within, as exemplified by W.B. Riley's (failed) crusade in the Northern Baptist Convention.

Instead, the Riley-led WCFA turned its attention from eliminating modernism from the denominations to removing evolution from public schools, state universities, and church colleges. This was certainly a natural move for Riley, given that, as noted above, as early as 1909 Riley had concluded that evolution was a lethal threat to church and society. In the 1920s Riley published a number of pieces dealing with this topic, including the two pamphlets mentioned above. He also wrote *Inspiration or Evolution?*, which eventually went through three editions, and which included two chapters that were also printed as pamphlets (and are included in this volume): *The Theory of Evolution—Does It Tend to Anarchy?* (192?); and *The Theory of Evolution—Does It Tend to Atheism?* (192?)

In the spring of 1922 Riley, in the official WCFA periodical, *Christian Fundamentals in School and Church,* published an editorial entitled "The Evolution Controversy!" An opening salvo in the antievolution crusade, this brief piece neatly summarizes Riley's argument against the teaching of evolution. He begins by asserting that the "first and most important reason for its elimination [from the classroom] is in the unquestioned fact that evolution is not a science; it is a hypothesis only, a speculation."[3] Riley makes this point repeatedly, obsessively, in his writings; for Riley, and for other fundamentalist antievolutionists, science was defined in a very commonsensical way: "knowledge gained and verified by exact observation and correct thinking." Evolution, a "theory," a mere collection of suppositions and guesses, failed to meet this standard. The requisite supporting evidence simply did not exist: evolutionists could provide no proof that life can originate from nothing, nor could they give a single example of "one species actually evolving into another."[4]

Not only was evolution unscientific, but, as Riley goes on to argue in "The Evolution Controversy!," the theory "doesn't harmo-

*Introduction* *xiii*

nize with Scripture."⁵ Whatever modernists might say, the Genesis account of creation and *Origin of Species* simply could not be reconciled. More than this, there was "an utter inharmony between evolution and the Christian faith." As Riley saw it, to accept evolution was to abandon the fundamentals of the Christian faith. As Riley asserted in 1925, the evidence of this point was overwhelming: "there is not in America today one living minister who holds at the same time to the evolutionary hypothesis and to the full inspiration of the Bible, the very deity of Christ, and the blood atonement."⁶ In fact, as Riley underscores in his pamphlet *The Theory of Evolution—Does It Tend to Atheism?*, to accept evolutionism was to move toward seeing God as an impersonal force, or even rejecting God altogether.

This said, Riley was also at great pains, as were his antievolutionist compatriots, to make clear that the Bible was perfectly congruent with "true science." Many of Riley's antievolutionist writings, including a number of pamphlets in this volume, sought to demonstrate that the best scientific research confirms the veracity of the Biblical record. Riley pointed out in a 1925 article that biology has revealed that the first chapter of Genesis is correct in noting that each species produces "after its kind"; that geology has demonstrated that the "order of creation is exactly that found" in Genesis; and that all the sciences provide proof of the fact that, as noted in Genesis 1, God has given humans "lordship of the earth and all that is in it."⁷

Regarding the Genesis creation account, it should be noted that William Bell Riley held to a "day-age" theory. That is, Riley believed that "the days of Genesis are aeons, ages, geological days, days of God and not days of men."⁸ He briefly makes this argument in the pamphlet *The Scientific Accuracy of the Sacred Scriptures* (contained in this volume). A much fuller articulation of his day-age views came in a friendly 1929 debate with fellow antievolutionist Harry Rimmer, in which Riley asserted that "if we consider the progressive character of creation as found in nature, creative days [periods] are argued; if we consider the testimony of geology, creative days are absolutely demanded." That Riley held such a view is a significant example of the point that Ronald Numbers has argued: until the last few decades most creationists "readily conceded that the Bible allowed for an ancient earth and pre-Edenic life."⁹ (That Riley may have changed his mind on this point is also significant—see below.)

Riley opposed the teaching of evolution because it was both unscientific and un-Christian. But it is interesting to note that Riley often devoted the most attention and the most passion to evolutionism's dreadful social impact. This was certainly true in the aforementioned editorial, "The Evolution Controversy!" In this piece Riley, as he often did in the 1920s, used Germany as his example: the Germans' acceptance of the idea of "the survival of the fittest" led them to believe that they had the right to expand their boundaries and increase their power, without regard for the rights of neighboring nations. The result was "war, with all its attendant iniquities," including "the world's financial and moral bankruptcy." Unfortunately for the world, the Great War would not be the last of Darwinism's "baneful effects." As more people accepted the evolutionary philosophy, as more people came to see themselves as merely animals "in a higher state of development," as more people came to deny their divine origins, the result would be that "the moral foundations on which the greatest of the world's modern states rest, can no longer be retained against the rising tide of this so-called science, but will be swept out of their places, gnarled, twisted, torn, and finally flung on the banks of time's tide."[10] (For even more vivid descriptions of the social impact of evolution, see Riley's pamphlet, *The Theory of Evolution—Does It Tend to Anarchy?*)

In response to this threat facing both church and society, in the early 1920s William Bell Riley led his World's Christian Fundamentals Association to war against the evolutionists. One part of this fight involved the organization's president in verbal duels with the enemy. Riley challenged any and all comers to debate the merits of the issue. While some prominent proponents of evolutionism (e.g., Clarence Darrow) ducked the combative WCFA president (in the process incurring Riley's public ridicule), others took him up on his challenge, including Edward Adams Cantrell of the American Civil Liberties Union; English rationalist Joseph McCabe; Charles Smith, president of the American Association for the Advancement of Atheism; and Maynard Shipley, president of the Science League of America.

Debating Riley must have been a disconcerting experience for many of Riley's opponents, particularly for those individuals who assumed that they would be engaging in an academic disputation. Riley's first debate, in May, 1922, is illustrative. Riley was scheduled to lead a WCFA Bible conference in Raleigh, North Carolina. On the morning of his arrival he read in the paper an article written by six North Carolina State College professors, in which they "savagely disputed" the fundamentalist claim that evolution was antithetical to the Christian faith. Riley immediately sent a message to all six professors, challenging them to a public debate. When they did not respond, Riley began making phone calls;

## Introduction

finally, one of the professors, biologist Z.P. Metcalf, agreed to go up against Riley.[11] The debate was held in the college's Pullen Hall, which was jammed to capacity. Actually, in many ways it was more of a sporting event than a debate; as a local reporter noted, for "a full hour and a half the crowd that jammed the hall ... yelled and whistled, clapped their hands, and pounded the floor with their feet." Metcalf read a scholarly paper, establishing in some detail the geological and biological evidence for evolution. Then it was Riley's turn. He did not deliver a prepared speech. Instead, to quote the reporter on the scene, he relied upon his crowd-pleasing "ability as a ready speaker": "Dr. Riley shifted the attack with bewildering movement, at one moment reciting an anecdote that left his supporters howling ... and the next delivering some cryptic indictment with sharp, incisive sentences." At "one point he picked up a volume on evolution, and turned to some pictures of pre-historic men. He made to do about pronouncing their names, ridiculed them, [and said:] 'Come up here after the debate and look at these pictures, and I am sure you will see somebody who looks just like them when you get down town.'"[12]

When the debate was over, Riley pressed Metcalf to permit a vote of the audience on the question. While in this instance Metcalf demurred, such "rising votes" would become a hallmark of Riley debates. Given his skills in verbal combat, and given that he often packed the audience with sympathetic fundamentalists, it is not surprising that most of Riley's twenty-eight debates resulted in substantial majorities for the indomitable Baptist preacher. His triumphs certainly gave him and his supporters no end of satisfaction. At the age of 84 he was still gloating over his victories: "I sincerely regret that its [evolutionism's] advocates decided to abandon the field of debate; I cannot blame them!"[13]

In the crusade against evolution William Bell Riley was not simply interested in debating the enemy. He also wanted his World's Christian Fundamentals Association to become politically mobilized, the goal being to make illegal the teaching of evolution in America's public schools. As Riley noted in the winter of 1923, it was imperative that good Christians unite to stop unscrupulous educators from their deadly task of surreptitiously spreading the "tares of evolution": "There are hundreds of teachers whose hands ought to be stayed from this broad-casting, and hundreds of text books that ought to be excluded before their teachings take root in the garden of the Lord, the Home, ... the Church and the World." To those who might object, on grounds of "free thought and free speech," to such a campaign on the part of the World's Christian Fundamentals Association, Riley responded:

"let the parent and tax payer, whose most vital interests—children—are being injured" remind critics "that where our fence is built and our fields begin, infidel liberties end!"[14]

In response to Riley's call, by 1923 the WCFA had organized campaigns throughout the United States, hoping to put enough public pressure on state legislators that they would ban the teaching of evolution in their particular state. Riley himself led the WCFA troops into a number of Southern states. One of those states was Tennessee, where, in early 1925, the state legislature passed an antievolution bill.

When John Thomas Scopes and the American Civil Liberties Union challenged the Tennessee statute, Riley immediately decided that the World's Christian Fundamentals Association must become involved in what could be an important test case. At the 1925 convention, which was held, quite appropriately, in Memphis, the WCFA passed a resolution pledging its support of the state of Tennessee in defending its "righteous law." In particular, "the organization 'propose[d] to employ one of the most capable of living attorneys . . . in behalf of our Association and in the interests of both Christianity and American civilization,' promising him 'whatever support is needful to . . . conserve the righteous law of the Commonwealth of Tennessee.'"[15]

Of course, the attorney referred to in the WCFA resolution was William Jennings Bryan. Given's Bryan's antievolution activities and national prominence, he was a natural choice. According to Riley, Bryan "agreed immediately" to Riley's request (although he did decline the WCFA offer of compensation). Yet Riley, who made much of the fact that he took the lead in opposing Scopes, and who made much of his role in securing Bryan for the prosecution, did not attend the trial. Bryan implored him to be there; Riley, however, was caught up in the fight over doctrinal requirements for Northern Baptist missionaries, and hence instead attended the denominational convention in Seattle (a useful reminder that Riley's fundamentalist exertions always involved more than antievolution). From afar Riley concluded that Bryan had won a *"signal conquest"* (emphasis his), convincing not only judges and jurors, but also "an intelligent world." As Riley saw it, the antievolutionists' victory was marred by only two things: first, unfair press coverage on the part of "disgusting blood-suckers" who themselves were "steeped" in evolutionism; and second, Bryan's death soon after the trial. But regarding the latter, Riley saw a silver lining: "The cause in behalf of which he had sacrificed his life, fundamentalism, took fresh hold upon the earth, new faith being engendered, and new friends being instantly raised up."[16]

## Introduction

In this regard Riley could have been referring to the flurry of WCFA antievolution activities immediately after the Scopes trial. As far as he was concerned, the most important of these efforts took place in Minnesota; in fact, the antievolution crusade in Riley's home state marks the high point of his antievolution activities.

In 1923 Riley had created the Minnesota Anti-Evolution League, which had as its goal the elimination of "the teaching of the unproven evolutionary hypothesis . . . from the tax-supported schools," particularly given that this "theory is constantly being made the occasion of opposition to Scripture, and often of scoffing the Christian faith."[17] But the League did little in its early years. It was not until 1926 that Riley went on the attack. The spark was a decision by University of Minnesota administrators not to allow Riley to give an antievolution address on campus. Infuriated, Riley responded by renting the nearby Kenwood Armory. On March 7, with over 5,000 people in attendance, Riley gave a riproaring speech, in which he blasted the school's administration for inculcating students with an atheistic "philosophy masquerading as a science," and in which he called on those in attendance to join with the Anti-Evolution League in "demand[ing] that the University which belongs to us all . . . not become the personal property of a dozen regents or a hundred Darwinized or Germanized, deceived and faithless professors!"[18]

Encouraged by the public support he received, Riley decided the time was ripe for a state antievolution law. He drafted a bill, which was introduced into the state legislature, prohibiting all tax-supported educational institutions (including the University of Minnesota) from "teaching that mankind either descended or ascended from a lower order of animals." In an effort to increase popular pressure on the legislators, Riley and other WCFA speakers (including Gerald Winrod) crisscrossed the state, speaking in over 200 towns about the evils of evolution and the virtues of Riley's bill. On March 8, 1927, almost one year to the day after his dramatic speech at the armory, Riley concluded his campaign with a speech in the state legislature. But his address, in which he claimed that his bill was popular with college undergraduates (if not their professors), was undercut by the revelation that 6,500 University of Minnesota students had signed a petition against the proposed antievolution law. The next day the vote was taken. The Riley bill was overwhelmingly defeated, 55 to 7.

Afterward Riley bravely proclaimed that the Minnesota fight was only the first skirmish of the battle to outlaw the teaching of evolution.[19] But the reality was that this dismal failure was a crushing blow to Riley's national antievolution crusade. The Minnesota experience proved that, outside the South, there was little enthusiasm for legislation on the order of Riley's bill; to many folks such a law seemed a grave threat to the separation of church and state. In short, except for some work in Arkansas in 1928, the Minnesota debacle signalled the end of William Bell Riley's efforts to secure antievolution legislation.

In a larger sense it signalled the end of Riley's national fundamentalist crusade. With the collapse of the antievolution effort Riley's World's Christian Fundamentals Association shrunk, then slipped into oblivion; Riley himself quit the WCFA presidency in 1929. Over the next two decades Riley concentrated much of his energies at the local and regional level. Much of his work involved Northwestern Bible School, which he had started in 1902 with seven students in a tiny room in his First Baptist Church. By 1946 the Northwestern Schools (Bible School, College, and Seminary) enrolled 700 day and 1,000 evening students; more than this, Northwestern had become the center of a regional fundamentalist enterprise, providing pastors, church workers, and religious literature for a network of conservative churches throughout the upper Midwest. In effect, Riley presided over a regional fundamentalist empire, a role that allowed him and his fundamentalist allies (many of whom were Northwestern graduates) to capture control of the Minnesota Baptist Convention in the late 1930s.

Besides working to advance fundamentalism in the upper Midwest, Riley devoted much energy in the 1930s to propagating an anti-Semitic, conspiratorial theory of world events. Borrowing heavily from the infamous *Protocols of the Elders of Zion,* Riley asserted, in numerous pamphlets and articles, that the international Jewish-Bolshevik cabal was steadily, covertly working to grasp control of the world's governments and finances, toward that day when the "king despot of Zion" would control the world. While it was obvious that the conspiracy was at work in America, controlling both the media and Franklin Roosevelt's collectivist New Deal, the *"Protocol* plan" was most advanced in the Soviet Union, where Jew-Bolsheviks had fully implemented their program (which included state-controlled socialism and state-imposed atheism). According to Riley, the one world leader who correctly understood the threat posed by the Jewish conspiracy was Germany's Adolf Hitler, who heroically worked to foil the Jews' nefarious plot.

What is important is that Riley perceived evolutionism to be an integral part of the Jewish conspiratorial program. Through "his study of the Bolshevik rule of Russia," Riley concluded that the Jewish bosses had simply shifted from "GOD to gorilla," applying "the philsophy of Darwin . . . to politics in the enslavement or even murder" of their opponents. In the United States the Jewish conspiracy, which "largely controls our higher education today," was aggressively promoting evolutionism in the classroom. And on a personal note, in a 1936 sermon Riley bitterly noted that, not surprisingly, it was "young atheist Jews" who were his "most annoying hecklers" when he was out on the stump lecturing against evolution.[20]

There is no evidence that Riley, who died in 1947, ever abandoned his belief in an international Jewish-Bolshevik-Darwinist conspiracy. On the other hand, perhaps in response to the threat of government prosecution, after 1940 Riley did cease to defend Hitler. In fact, in 1941 Riley published *Hitlerism: or, The Philosophy of Evolution in Action*, which is included in this volume, and which is remarkably similar to Riley's attacks on Darwinized Germany two decades earlier.

While much of his work after 1930 was devoted to building a regional fundamentalist empire and propagating anti-Semitic conspiratorialism, in the 1930s and 1940s Riley continued to deliver sermons and write articles and tracts in which he fervently attacked the weaknesses and evils of evolution. Besides *Hitlerism*, four antievolution pamphlets from these years are included in this volume: *Are the Scriptures Scientific?* (1936); *Darwin's Philosophy and the Flood* (193?); *Evolution—A False Philosophy* (193?); and *The Theory of Evolution Tested by Mathematics* (193?).

One point needs to be made regarding Riley's antievolutionism in these years: he may have been moving away from the day-age theory he advocated in the 1920s and toward George McCready Prices's flood geology, which limits life on earth to about six thousand years. There is some negative evidence in this regard. In *Are the Scriptures Scientific?*, a revised (and more strident) version of his 1920 pamphlet *The Scientific Accuracy of the Sacred Scriptures*, Riley completely excised the section dealing with the day-age theory. On the positive side, in his pamphlet *Darwin's Philosophy and the Flood* Riley repeats many of the arguments advanced by Price, including arguments that bear directly on the notion that there has been life on earth for only a few thousand years. While Price's name is not mentioned in this pamphlet, in a later article Riley gives him his due, noting that "some of us believe that the enigma of geology," including the coal beds and the marks on the rocks that were erroneously credited to the ice age, "will never be explained until Price's theory on flood geology is accepted."[21]

It would be nice to argue here that William Bell Riley embodies the recent, dramatic shift in creationism away from, to quote Ronald Numbers, "theories that allowed the history of life on earth to span millions of years to a doctrine . . . that compressed earth history into no more than ten thousand years." But it must be noted that many of the early antievolutionists promoted Price's ideas without really understanding that flood geology was incompatible with concepts such as the day-age theory.[22] This may apply to Riley: while he removed the "day-age section" from *Are the Scriptures Scientific?*, in that very same pamphlet he refers to Genesis days as "creative periods" that correspond with geological ages, language that certainly conjures up Riley's defense of a day-age theory of creation, whatever his sympathies with flood geology.

When Riley wrote against evolution, he was more interested in scoring points against the enemy than in maintaining logical consistency in his argument. Even if he had been so inclined, Riley would have been hard-pressed to maintain a coherent antievolution argument, given that he was not a scientist, or even moderately informed in the sciences. But that is not the point. Riley believed in his bones that evolution was a dangerous threat to church, society, and the world. For that reason he wrote and spoke against evolution for four decades. What matters most about William Bell Riley the antievolutionist is that, as perhaps the most important fundamentalist leader of his generation, no one did more to tie the fundamentalist movement to antievolutionism. This legacy remains with us today.

## NOTES

1. For a more complete discussion of Riley's career, from which some of this essay is derived, see William Vance Trollinger, Jr., *God's Empire: William Bell Riley and Midwestern Fundamentalism* (Madison: University of Wisconsin Press, 1990), esp. chs. 2–3.
2. William Bell Riley, *The Great Divide; or, Christ and the Present Crisis* (Philadelphia: Bible Conference Committee, 1919): 3.
3. [William Bell Riley], "The Evolution Controversy!," *Christian Fundamentals in School and Church* 4(April–June, 1922): 5.
4. William Bell Riley, "The World's Christian Fundamentals Association and the Scopes Trial," *Christian Fundamentals in School*

Introduction                                                                 xxi

and Church 7(October–December, 1925): 40–42. Regarding fundamentalists and their definition of science, see George Marsden, *Fundamentalism and American Culture: The Shaping of Twentieth-Century Evangelicalism, 1870-1925* (New York: Oxford University Press, 1980), 19–20, 214–15; and Ronald L. Numbers, *The Creationists* (New York: Knopf, 1992), 50–53.

5. "The Evolution Controversy!," 6.
6. William Bell Riley, "Bryan, the Great Commoner and Christian," *Christian Fundamentals in School and Church* 7(October–December 1925): 10. This point about the conflict between evolutionism and orthodox Christianity is central to *The Finality of the Higher Criticism* and *Inspiration or Evolution?*
7. Riley, "WCFA and the Scopes Trial," 46–47.
8. William Bell Riley and Harry Rimmer, *A Debate: Resolved, that the Creative Days in Genesis Were Aeons, Not Solar Days* (n.p., 1929), 6.
9. Riley and Rimmer, *Debate*, 16; Numbers, *The Creationists*, x.
10. "The Evolution Controversy!" 5.
11. Marie Acomb Riley, *The Dynamic of a Dream: The Life Story of Dr. William B. Riley* (Grand Rapids, MI: Wm. B. Eerdmans, 1938), 110–111.
12. "Dr. W.B. Riley of Minneapolis and Dr. Z.P. Metcalf of Raleigh State College in Debate," *Christian Fundamentals in School and Church* 4(July–September 1922): 11–15.
13. William Bell Riley, "The Sickly Birth of Evolution," *The Northwestern Pilot* 26(October, 1945):3.
14. William Bell Riley, "Shall We Tolerate Longer the Teaching of Evolution?," *Christian Fundamentals in School and Church* 5 (January–March 1923): 82–86.
15. Riley, "WCFA and the Scopes Trial," 37–28.
16. Riley, "Bryan, the Great Commoner and Christian," 5–11, 37.
17. "Organization of Anti-Evolution League," *Christian Fundamentals in School and Church* 5 (January–March 1923): 66–67.
18. "Riley Assails 'U' As Fostering State Atheism," *Minneapolis Tribune*, March 8, 1926.
19. Ferenc Morton Szasz, "William B. Riley and the Fight Against Teaching of Evolution in Minnesota," *Minnesota History* 41(Spring 1969): 201–16.
20. M.A. Riley, *Dynamic*, 188; William Bell Riley, *Protocols and Communism* (Minneapolis: L.W. Camp, 1934), 14; William Bell Riley, sermon given at the First Baptist Church, Minneapolis, Minn., October 18, 1936, reported by Charles I. Cooper and S.W., Box 54: "Subversive Activities: Minnesota, 1936," Jewish Community Re-

lations Council of Minnesota Papers, Minnesota State Historical Society, St. Paul, Minn.
21. William Bell Riley, "Prophecy and Past History," *The Northwestern Pilot* 26(Nov. 1945): 57.
22. Numbers, *The Creationists,* x–xi, 96–101.

# Are the Scriptures Scientific?

by
W. B. RILEY, D.D.

## NEW BOOKS BY DR. RILEY

| | | |
|---|---|---|
| Pastoral Problems | Cloth | $1.50 |
| Youth's Victory Lies This Way | Cloth | 1.00 |
| The Only Hope of Church or World | Cloth | .75 |
| Will Christ Come Again? (4th edition) | Cloth | 1.00 |

## OTHER VOLUMES BY THE AUTHOR

| | | |
|---|---|---|
| Revival Sermons | Cloth | $1.50 |
| | Paper | .75 |
| Inspiration or Evolution | Cloth | 1.25 |
| | Pager | .60 |
| Perennial Revival | Cloth | 1.50 |
| | Paper | .75 |
| Modernism, or The Blight of Unitarianism | Paper | .50 |
| The Philosophies of Father Coughlin | Paper | .25 |
| The Menace of Modernism | Paper | .40 |
| Ephesians—The Threefold Epistle | Paper | .50 |

# Are the Scriptures Scientific?

by

*W. B. Riley, D.D.*

"*Thy word is true from the beginning.*"—Ps. 119:160.

To raise this question "Are the Scriptures Scientific?" brings a smile to the face of the skeptic, but it gives to the true student occasion of study. The believer accepts without controversy the Psalmist's statement concerning God's Book—"*Thy word is true from the beginning.*" The unbeliever instantly rejects it, but the unprejudiced student only demands evidence for the assertion.

To this, intelligent Christians take no exception. If the Bible will not bear investigation, if scrutiny discloses shortcomings, if research disproves its assertions, if true science discredits its clear claims, it should fall. We could forfeit it without a tear; join in digging its grave without regret, and return to the duties of life smitten by no serious bereavement.

But the men best informed upon this subject have little alarm lest that should be the fate of the most revered Book. They contend rather that Scripture and Science are harmonious and that any imaginary conflict between them is only the nightmare of uninformed minds. Holding that God is the author of the Bible and that He is also the Creator of the natural universe, they stand ready to furnish proofs of perfect agreement between God's Word and God's work.

Many years ago, and before I had entered upon a series of debates against the proponents of Evolution, a co-laborer in our Northwestern Theological School,—Dr. A. J. Frost—a Senior in years and a man of intellect quite as massive as his gigantic body, gave me this advice:—"If you ever have occasion to debate, insist upon the definition of the terms involved. Definition results in definiteness and lays some limitations upon the parties involved."

We propose now a similar procedure, and pass to

# THE DEFINITION OF TERMS

The subjects of our present concern are Scriptures and Science.

## The Standard Dictionary Defines Science

It is "knowledge gained and verified by exact observation and correct thinking; especially as methodically formulated and arranged in a rational system."

That definition takes you at once out of the realm of speculation; it disposes of such terms as "theory," "assumption," "hypothesis," making them possible servants of science, but never its synonyms.

A hundred years ago we had our sciences so-called, but today the most of them sleep in the Morgue of Speculation. The explanation is easy; — "The verification of knowledge by exact observation and correct thinking" is the highest compliment of which the human mind is capable. Not every man who cries "Eureka" has found it.

This is not to inveigh against the sincerity of investigators nor to suggest a cessation from their researches, nor even to reject all their conclusions, but only to call attention to the difficulties that beset their way and warn against the too-oft repeated mistake of identifying science with "speculation" or "theory" or "hypothesis," as has so often and so falsely been done with the guess of Evolution.

"Knowledge gained and verified by exact observation and correct thinking" will never be overthrown by mortal man, nor even by God Himself.

### An Inspired Apostle Defines Scripture.

*"All scripture is given by inspiration of God, and is profitable for doctrine, for reproof, for correction, for instruction in righteousness:"*

(II Tim. 3:16)

Paul speaks of *"all Scripture"* as that which is *"God-breathed,"* and the method of its arrival was that *"holy men of God spake as they were moved* (or borne along) *by the Holy Ghost."* (II Peter 1:21).

Conscious of belonging himself to that inspired company, Paul affirms, — *"Which things also we speak, not in the words which man's wisdom teacheth, but which the Holy Ghost teacheth;"* (I Cor. 2:13).

We confess very frankly that

this passage seems to us to agree with hundreds of others in confirming the verbal inspiration of the Bible. College students know that many professors now strongly inveigh against that doctrine; and, even though they belong to the professed Christian company, they propagate another theory altogether, admitting that God may have "stimulated" the thought, but objecting to his having provided "words" with which to clothe it.

The Verbal Inspiration theory these now commonly set aside, and the doctrine of "illumination" is advocated instead as the most that can be claimed for the authors of the sixty-six books that constitute this great Library.

The same men, however, who reject the Bible as the very Word of God, would go into Court tomorrow and insist upon the settlement of an Estate in which they were named as heirs, on a verbal basis, and would call the attention of attorneys and judge to *"what was written"* and, unless they had some unrighteous end to be conserved, they would permit no departure from the very words in which the testator had expressed himself.

It is little wonder, therefore, that

the New Testament writers, who may be conceded to have known what the Scriptures were, refer to the Old Testament more than eighty times as that *"which is written;"* and never once did they abandon the literal acceptance of the same.

The modern method of admitting that the Bible may "contain" the Scriptures, but is not itself "wholly God's word," is merely a form of unbelief. If God has revealed His will to men in this Book it is hardly reasonable that He would do so with less care than any intelligent, faithful father would show in framing the document that bequeathed his possessions to his children. If, in the Civil Courts, the slightest word of the testator is the weightiest law, who would dare to treat with contempt thought or phrase found in the Divine WILL?

Let it be understood there is a decided difference between the plain statement of Sacred Scripture and some absurd interpretation. The scientist is under no obligation whatever to harmonize "knowledge gained and verified" with fanciful interpretations of Holy Writ; nor is the intelligent student of Scripture under the slightest obligation to bring the Bible into line with the pseudo-sciences of the day. Science is God's voice in nature, and the Scriptures are God's voice in Grace. It does not fall to the lot of any mortal to harmonize these voices; the harmony is in Him.

### This Common Authorship Compels Agreement

With man, that would not be a logical necessity! Man can, and often does, write and speak contradictory things.

It is said that an auditor once went to Mr. Beecher and said:—"Dr. Beecher, what you said today was contradictory to what you said last Sunday." To which Beecher is reported to have replied:—"Come and hear me next Sunday and you may find I will contradict the statements of both days."

But such controversion is not consonant with the character of God.

"*** *He abideth faithful: he cannot deny himself.*" (II Tim. 2: 13).

On more than one occasion I have heard liberal theologians discuss the subject of "Harmony Between Science and Scripture" and apparently, to their personal satisfaction, accomplish the same by quietly dismissing the claims of the Sacred Book with a waive of the hand or a jerk of the head, saying, for instance, of Moses and other early writers—"They faithfully recorded the views of their day, but Science has long since discredited such primitive impressions."

Is that harmony? Is it not, rather, annihilation? It may let you out of your difficulty, but you escape at the expense of inspiration, and to the unspeakable loss of the people.

There used to be an eccentric preacher in Kentucky well-known to the author. He did no great amount of study, and yet he commonly preached with unction. One day he found himself before an audience with no unction on hand; even thoughts refused to come. He floundered through a few ill-formed sentences, and then, squarely facing his audience, he said:— "Brethren and sisters; you think I have got into the brush and can't get out, don't you? Well, I'll show you; we'll just look to the Lord and be dismissed!"

But let it be understood that when you dismiss the claims of the Sacred Book and walk out of your difficulties, you have lost the Divine message and left the hungry multitudes unsatisfied.

However, these three primal remarks but introduce—

## THE THINGS OF DEBATE

Frankly we enter upon that without the least fear. God's Holy Book has lived through a war of several thousand years; and, instead of wearying with the battle, it is more virile and combative today than ever before. Defeat is not in God's dictionary. To the conflict then!

We concede that

### Genesis Is the Storm Center of This Controversy.

That has come largely in consequence of Charles Darwin's work on "THE ORIGIN OF SPECIES." The ancient author of the Pentateuch and the modern philosopher of Evolution are in direct conflict. The so-called Liberals of the day follow Darwin: Conservative scholars consent with Moses.

The reason for the course of the latter is found in the fact that, to this good hour, not one statement of that matchless chapter—Genesis 1:—has been shown to be unscientific.

In demonstration of this declaration, let us take the statements up in their order:—

*First* — *"In the beginning God created the heaven and the earth."* (Gen. 1:1).

Here two questions of Science are involved. The source of the physical universe; and The order of Origins.

Beyond controversy Sir William Thomson, or Lord Kelvin, was, in the realm of science, without a superior in his day. Concerning the origin of the Universe he said:

"Science positively affirms creative power."

Among modern astronomers, James Jeans knows no superior; and yet he does not hesitate to speak of "the Creator" and of "Creation"; and while he does not use the Biblical term "God," he does say: "The great architect of the Universe now begins to appear as a pure mathematician." The views of Professor Millikan are well known to the scientific world, and Jeans quotes him as having said of creation:—"The Creator is still on the job."

Again, the order of creation as set forth here is that now uniformly accepted by scientists, namely, so far as our section of the universe is concerned the heavenly bodies were created first and the earth afterwards. In other words, the old geocentric system which looked upon the earth as the center of the universe, had to give place to the heliocentric system which, for thousands of years after Moses, was held by supposed scientists; but into their mistake Moses never fell.

It is doubtful if there is a scientist living who would deny that at one time *"the earth was without form, and void; and darkness was upon the face of the deep."* (Gen. 1:2).

The statement of Gen. 1:3—"* * * *Let there be light and there was light"*—before the rays of the sun, on the fourth day of creation, had reached the earth, was at one time disputed; but finally Laplace appeared declaring it to be a scientific certainty, that, in the condensation of the originally formless chaos, there was such molecular and chemical action as must have emitted light! No truth-seeker arose to dispute him, and Boardman in his "Creative Week" remarked,— "Why will the Academy vote Moses a blunderer for declaring that light existed before the sun appeared, and yet vote Laplace a scientist for affirming precisely the same thing?"

Take the 5th verse:—*"And God called the light Day, and the darkness he called Night."*

Till now the language of science has not departed from this statement.

*"And God said, Let there be a firmament in the midst of the waters, and let it divide the waters from the waters.*

*"And God made the firmament, and divided the waters which were under the firmament from the waters which were above the firmament: and it was so.*

*"And God called the firmament Heaven."* (6-8).

Huxley is reputed to have slipped here by charging Moses with believing that heaven was a solid substance, resting like a canopy over the earth. But Huxley's mistake was the result of his ignorance of Hebrew, since the word translated into the Latin "firmamentum" is the Hebrew word "rakiah," correctly translated *"a broad expanse."*

How significant!—*"A broad expanse"!* The present-day scientist will tell you that that *"expanse"* is so broad that they know not whether it be finite or infinite; so broad

14

that though Jeans insists that the only thing with which we are familiar that can compare in number with the stars are the sands of the sea; and yet, innumerable as those stars are, and enormous in size, almost past human computation this broad expanse, instead of being insufferably crowded, Jeans declares to be emptier than anything we can imagine and then illustrates by saying:—

"Leave only three wasps alive in the whole of Europe and the air of Europe will still be more crowded with wasps than space is with stars."

And as for the waters which were in the heavens and the waters that are on the earth, modern science has again justified Moses by telling us that there is a veritable sea forever suspended in the first heavens by the law of evaporation! If any man doubt it, let him express his skepticism to dwellers along the Ohio River or the Mississippi valley who lately had the scientific demonstration of seeing oceans of it fall from the firmament above to the firmament below.

But still further:—

*"And God said, Let the waters under the heaven be gathered to-*

*gether unto one place, and let the dry land appear: and it was so.*

*"And God called the dry land Earth; and the gathering together of the waters called he Seas: and God saw that it was good."*

(Gen. 1:9-10).

That statement used to be laughed at as a further sign of Moses' ignorance, supposing that he had seen but one sea and imagined it the only one on earth! But now exploration has turned the laugh on Moses' critics, for it has proven, as Dana in his "Manual of Geology" tells us that while "the continents are separated, the seas occupy one bed."

Here is wisdom that is wonderful!

Proceeding now to the Acts of Creation we find a remarkable agreement between Genesis and Geology. They both begin with *grass* as the oldest form of life and come up through *herbs, trees, fish, fowl, living creatures, cattle, and creeping things,* and *beasts of the earth* to *man* as the last and most wonderful of God's creations.

There is not a mistake from the standpoint of the geologist in this arranged system. The very rocks bear testimony to the Divinity of this revelation.

I have found it extremely interesting to compare Genesis and Geology at other points. There are mentioned in the 1st chapter of Genesis three creative periods relating themselves to life upon the earth, called the Third Day, the Fifth Day and the Sixth Day of Divine work.

I consult my Dictionary and find it also recognizes three creative periods,—Paleozoic, Mesozoic and Zenozoic.

Is this a coincidence?

When I turn back to the specimens found in these three periods I discover that they are all quite clearly included in the Genesis account.

But I must pause a moment to remark on the almost unthinkable wisdom found in the Fourth Day procedure where, not the earth, but the heavens are the subject of consideration.

*"And God made two great lights; the greater light to rule the day, and the lesser light to rule the night:* \* \* \*

*"And God set them in the firmament of the heaven to give light upon the earth."* (16-17).

On this let me make two or three observations that should at least impress the most confirmed skeptic.

First of all the word "made" is not "bara"—which implies a creative act, but "asa" — a Hebrew word that suggests appointment to function. There is, therefore, no harmony between Genesis 1:1 where God created the heavens and 1:16 where He appointed the sun and the moon *"to rule over the day and over the night."*

More remarkable still is the statement — *"the greater light to rule the day, and the lesser light to rule the night."*

How did Moses find out that the Sun was bigger than the Moon? He had no instruments with which to affect their measure, and all the appearances were to the contrary. I have seen the rising Moon when six to eight feet seemed to be its diameter, and the setting Moon under similar conditions; but three or four feet at the most would commonly compass the rising Sun, or the Sun at set.

The Greeks, therefore, following natural reason, believed that the dimness of the Moon was due to its distance from the earth, and that it was the larger of the two heavenly lights; and just as naturally reasoned that the proximity of the Sun to the earth accounted for the warmth coming from that great center.

But now that modern science has mastered the subject, we find—in the language of Jeans,—that the Sun is not only 400 times as distant from the earth as the Moon, but it is also five million times as big as the Moon. Its diameter is about 400 times the Moon's diameter, or 109 times the earth's diameter; or 864,000 miles; and that no fewer than 1,300,000 earths could be packed inside its circumference.

Before these facts, clearly outlined in Genesis, let the critics come and humbly confess—not the mistakes of Moses, but of Bob Ingersoll and all skeptical confreres.

I will not at this time undertake to prove the very easily compassed proposition that man is a creation of God,—the climax of His work on earth and not an evolution from an amæba; that I have done so, often in other addresses and books obviates the necessity of repetition here.

I conclude as I began by saying that the first chapter of Genesis has weathered the storm, and comes out of the conflict with flying colors—its every proposition is now certified by the best scientists of the 20th Century.

## But, There Are Many Other Scriptures Involved in This Controversy

It is not within the province of this address to take up the asserted instances of conflict between science and Scripture, since that will be accomplished in a later chapter; but we here propose a marvelous demonstration of agreement instead.

In a recent class in Homiletics one of our Theological Seminary students presented an argument for the Inspiration of the Bible in which he said what can be abundantly proven, namely that the Divinity of the Book was strongly argued by the fact that the Bible was **historically** correct; no mistakes in its historic statements having yet been proven: that the Bible was **geographically** correct, — no dislocation of places having been discovered in its pages: that the Bible was **geologically** correct,— the first chapter of Genesis a demonstration: that the Bible was **botanically** correct,—the flowers mentioned in it can be found in Bible lands to this day and create a complete herbarium, satisfactory to any modern scientist: that the Bible was **astronomically** correct,—not only anticipating for our section of the universe the heliocentric system, but rightly naming and perfectly placing the stars it mentions, and even going so far as to call attention to the now conceded *"empty place in the North."*—

*"He stretcheth out the north over the empty place, and hangeth the earth upon nothing."* (Job 26:7).

He also presented an argument that the Bible is **physiologically** correct, and only modern discoveries have convinced us that man is *"wonderfully made"!*

*"I will praise thee; for I am fearfully and wonderfully made: * * *"* (Ps. 139:14).

When I read what the scientists have to say concerning the physical man I feel as I do when I follow Jeans in his vain endeavor to give me some hint of stars and space; I am staggered mentally! But if what they tell me is true, then the Psalmist's statement concerning the creation of his body is certainly justified.

If there be a thousand miles of blood vessels in my body, if there be 1,500,000 sweat glands on its surface, if my lungs are composed of 700,000,000 cells, if my heart beats for a single day were "concentrated into one huge throb of vital power, it would be sufficient to throw a ton of iron 120 feet into the air," then since it has already beat 3,000,000,000 times since I was born, and has lifted what would equal the weight of 600,000 tons, if my nervous system controlled by a brain that has 3,000,000,000,000 nerve cells of which 9,200,000,000 are in the cortex or covering of the brain alone, and if in my veins there are 30,000,000 white corpuscles and 180,000,000,000 red ones,—then it is some job for an amæba to evolute himself into that complexity, I grant! It sounds to me more like the work of God.

But we proceed: Having just spoken of those thousand miles of blood vessels, it is not out of order to remember the statement of Moses that *"life is in the blood."* —(Gen. 9:4).

Harvey, in 1628, discovered this same truth, and now it is uniformly accepted. Natural life is not in the flesh, not in the nerves, not in the brains, not in the bones, not in them all combined; it *"is in the blood."*

In Eccl. 1: we have rather clearly set forth two scientific facts which have been paraded in recent centuries as wonderful discoveries. The first belongs to the realm of the so-called Weather Bureau and tells us whence our storms or cold come, and also the source of heat winds; (vs. 6) and the second compasses the whole question of evaporation.

*"All the rivers run into the sea; yet the sea is not full."*

The reason is assigned here: *"Unto the place from whence the rivers come, thither they return again."* (vs. 7)

But perhaps nothing is more remarkable than the scientific statements to be found in the Book of Job. We have already referred to his reference to *"the empty place"* in the north. Our time forbids that I take up all the scientific suggestions of Job 38: Dr. Harry Rimmer in his volume "The Harmony of Science and Scripture" has well accomplished that job, and one stands amazed at their multitude!

But I do want to affirm that Job taught the rotundity, and the revolution on its axis, of the earth. (see 38:13)

Still more remarkable is this ancient's statement concerning the law of gravity. Other ancients had other methods of supporting the earth on mighty pillars, on the tusks of enormous elephants, on the back of Atlas; but into this folly the inspired writer never fell, for Job wrote:

*"He hangeth. the earth upon nothing"* (26:7)—the very deliverance of your latest science.

Even more astonishing still is the statement concerning wind and water. We still employ very unscientific speech when we declare a thing to be "as light as air," knowing that air has a pressure of 15 lbs. to the square inch; and we still talk as if the seas might be dried up, when science says there is no change, and the drops of water—so far as extent is concerned—being only simply a question as to whether it is in liquid or gaseous form.

But Job, anticipating the scientists by several thousand years, wrote:

*"To make the weight for the winds; and he weigheth the waters by measure"* (Job. 28:25).

Such instances of Scripture statement preceding scientific discoveries could be multiplied out of number; but I refrain in order to remark—*It is high time Pseudo-Scientists surrendered their skepticism.*

Refusal to be convinced when such facts face them reminds one of Æsop's favorite fables. You will remember that the wolf coming upon the lamb said to him:

"You are feeding upon my grass and I'm going to eat you for it;"

But the lamb replied: "Sir, I am but a babe, and have never tasted grass as yet. My mother's milk suffices for my food."

To which the wolf responded: "But you drank from my spring, and on that account I will eat you."

And again the lamb said: "No, Sir; I have not done so. My mother's milk is drink as well as food and I have never tasted water."

Whereupon the wolf replied:

"Well, anyway I'm not going to be cheated out of my meal"—and he started in to kill and consume.

Such a conduct ill becomes the professed scientist. He should be a searcher for truth and when "knowledge gained and verified" is presented to him he should have an open mind and be subject to conviction.

We pass now to

## THE UNDEBATABLE THEMES

There are Scripture subjects upon which science is silent.

There are points of human experience of which the microscope reveals nothing, the telescope tells nothing; they transcend scientific investigation. Tyndale admitted that the problem of the universe would never be solved.

And yet that problem is not so difficult from the scientific standpoint as are the problems of sin, substitution and salvation.

There have been many theories as to how sin came into the world; but if the Bible statements be rejected, the so-called scientific philosophy proves unsatisfactory. As Joseph Parker, the great City Temple, London, pastor once remarked, "the faintest scratch reveals the wolf in us."

Paul, whose experiences and observations on human life have seldom been exceeded, said:

*"Now the works of the flesh are manifest, which are these: Adultery, fornication, uncleanness, lasciviousness, idolatry, witchcraft, hatred, variance, emulations, wrath, strife, seditions, heresies, envyings, murders, drunkenness, revellings, and such like; of the which, I tell*

*you before, as I have also told you in time past, that they which do such things shall not inherit the kingdom of God"* (Gal. 5:19-21).

Jesus, admittedly the soundest Judge of human life the world ever saw, said:

*"Out of the heart proceed evil thoughts, murders, adulteries, fornications, thefts, false witness, blasphemies. These are the things which defile a man."*

For two thousand years, yea, for seven thousand, supposed scientists and professed philosophers have worked at the problem of sin and are as much at sea regarding the origin of sin, and as remote from the solution of the problem as they were when first they began.

The only light we have that has proven of value is that from the Sacred Word, and that found in Jesus of Nazareth, the Son of God. If this statement needs verification we can present a few millions of men and women whose experience attests its truthfulness; and in the last analysis, that is a scientific confirmation of Scripture. The multiplied experiences of men demonstrate the divinity of the Bible. Wherever this book has gone light has walked in its wake; morals have improved, and life itself has not only been made worthwhile, but both inspired and protected by its teachings.

A skeptic, in crossing Africa, found a native chieftain sitting calmly under a tree reading from a book. When asked what he was doing, he said, "Reading my Bible." "Why man," remarked the skeptic, "don't you know that that Book is out of date?"

"Maybe so in your country, but it is a good thing for you that it is not so in this, for had it been, we would have, some time since, made a meal of you."

It was James Russell Lowell, was it not, who said:

"When the microscopic search of skepticism, which has hunted the heavens and searched the seas to disprove the existence of a Creator, has turned its attention to human society, and has found a place on this planet ten miles square where a decent man can live in comfort and security, supporting and educating his children unspoiled and unpolluted; a place where age is reverenced, infancy respected, manhood appreciated, womanhood honored, and human life held in due regard—when skeptics can find such a place, ten miles square on this globe where the Gospel of

Christ has not gone and cleared the way and laid the foundation and made decency and security possible, it will then be in order for these skeptical *literati* to move thither, and there ventilate their views."

**There is a realm of the spirit that is superscientific.**

God does not come within the range of the modern telescope; revelation is not subject to the measurement of the modern yardstick, and spiritual experience is not to be investigated by the modern lense.

When the man who has been drunken for twenty years, and who, as a result, is a ragged, social outcast, staggers into a downtown mission and hears the Gospel and comes out never to drink again, supposed scientists will never be able to explain it; but that does not affect what you and I have often seen.

When a woman who has walked in the ways of wickedness is visited by a Christian sister and brought face to face with Scripture teaching until, under profound conviction, she cries, *"God be merciful to me a sinner"* and, after some minutes of weeping, rises with a face from which a new light shines, and declares that she has personally met the Redeemer and knows that her sins are pardoned, and gladly takes the path that *"shines more and more unto the perfect day"* the denials of the personality of the Spirit, or the experience of the soul, will never disregard what men and women have seen. They know that this Book contains the Gospel that has proven, and can prove, *"the power of God unto salvation";* and seeing that, they believe the Book divine.

One night in Paris, France, I was preaching and Dr. Reuben Saillens was my interpreter. I came to the close of a discourse upon this same subject, and I turned to Dr. Saillens and said, "Now, Dr., if you can put it into such French language as not to despoil its rhythm, I would like to close with a poem of which I am very fond," but concerning which I had seen again and again, "author unknown," and I started in.

At the end of my first line he was in a hearty laugh, and I could not imagine why my great friend should treat a poem of such portent so lightly. He divined my embarrassment and said, "Excuse me, Dr., but I assure you I can put that poem into French, since I wrote it myself some fifty years ago."

In his early life Saillens was a blacksmith, and from that experience he brought this poem:

"I paused one day beside the blacksmith's door
And listened to the anvil ring the evening's chime.
And looking in I saw upon the floor,
Old hammers, worn with beating years of time.

" 'How many anvils have you had,' said I,
'To wear and batter out these hammers so?'
'Just one,' he answered, with a twinkling eye,
'The anvil wears the hammers out, you know.'

"And so, I thought, the Anvil of God's Word
For ages skeptic blows have beat upon;
Yet, though the noise of infidel was heard
The anvil is unworn, the hammer's gone!"

We will bury more skeptics tomorrow, but the Book will abide, *"Forever Thy Word is settled in heaven."*

31

# The Bible of the Expositor and the Evangelist
### By W. B. Riley, D. D.

**A SET EVERY PREACHER WILL WANT!**

   39 volumes covering the entire Bible
   1 volume—index and addenda

   40 volumes, handsomely bound in black and gold

DEAR DR. RILEY:

"I have come absolutely to the conclusion that the best commentary and the best homiletic book on earth today is your series of books on 'Bible Exposition and Homiletics'—the series in which you cover the entire Bible. I get more out of it than I do all the books I have, put together."—

Rev. Luther Little, D.D., First Baptist Church, Charlotte, N. C.

```
40 volumes in cloth................$40.00
Paper set ........................ 20.00
One volume, cloth, post paid......  1.15
One volume, paper, post paid......   .60
```

Order of L. W. CAMP

1020 Harmon Place
Minneapolis, Minn.

# DARWINISM

## OR

# IS MAN A DEVELOPED MONKEY?

By

W. B. RILEY, D. D.

Minneapolis, Minn.

All rights reserved by the Author.

# IS MAN A DEVELOPED MONKEY?

## OR

# THE THEORY OF EVOLUTION AND FALSE THEOLOGY

---

A chapter from the volume, "The Theory of Evolution and False Theology," by W. B. Riley, D.D., Pastor First Baptist Church, Minneapolis, Minn.

"In the beginning God created the heavens and the earth. . . . And God said, Let the waters under the heavens be gathered together unto one place, and let the dry land appear: and it was so. . . . And God said, Let the earth put forth grass, herbs yielding seed, and fruit-trees bearing fruit after their kind, wherein is the seed thereof, upon the earth: and it was so. . . . And God said, Let the waters swarm with swarms of living creatures, and let birds fly above the earth in the open firmament of heaven. And God created the great sea-monsters, and every living creature that moveth, wherewith the waters swarmed, after their kind, and every winged bird after its kind; and God saw that it was good . . . And God said, Let the earth bring forth living creatures after their kind, cattle, and creeping things, and beasts of the earth, after their kind: and it was so. . . . And God said Let us make man in our image, after our likeness: and let them have the dominion over the fish of the sea, and over the birds of the heavens, and over the cattle, and over all the earth, and over every creeping thing that creepeth upon the earth. And God created man in his own image, in the image of God created he him; male and female created he them." Gen. 1:1, 9, 11, 20-21, 24, 26-27.

"By faith we understand that the worlds have been framed by the word of God, so that what is seen hath not been made out of things which appear." Heb. 11:3.

Our theme is "The Theory of Evolution and Theology." It may not have occurred to all that the theory of evolution and theology are indissolubly linked together. But every scientist understands, as do also intelligent teachers of the Scriptures, that the theory of evolution is not simply a question of the origin of species; but, in its present-day application, proposes to account for everything material, from fire-mist to the perfected frame of the universe; everything animated, from the fertilized cell of lowest life to the Man of Nazareth; and everything moral, from the sensation of an amoeba to the sacred communion between God and man.

When, therefore, a biologist says that the minister has nothing to do with the theory of evolution, he reveals either his ignorance of its applications or his indisposition to be disturbed by an adequate argument. When a professor in Natural Science says that people who are not constant students of his specialty should not pass any judgement upon its claims and contentions, he disputes the right of decision by a competent jury, and demands that the public close its eyes, that it may the more readily swallow his deliverances.

It may be necessary, therefore, for the man who decides to think for himself, and even maintain his right to judge the findings of so-called scientists, to "beg pardon"; but this formality performed, we pass on to question, compare, and conclude according to the individual judgement.

Every preacher of the present hour is compelled to deal with the theory of evolution, and either accept it or reject it. Its advocates have invaded his realm. Prof. Metcalf, biologist of the Woman's College, Baltimore, in his book "Organic Evolution" naively tells us that in coming to the position of a dignified science the last stronghold to be taken by evolution was that of the supernaturalist, "that of the man who claims that supernatural agency intervenes in nature in such a way as to modify the natural law of events." This opinion he thinks Darwin overthrew and doomed. (See "Introduction of Organic Evolution," p. 20.)

Such a suggestion clearly indicates that the entire company of conservative theologians are not only unscientific, but are mental mossbacks, clinging to exploded theories, preaching obsolete opinions and practicing doctrines long since out of date. If, therefore, one of them should fail to make an argument, the public ought not to be surprised. On the other hand, if he should succeed in making the theory of evolution look doubtful, it might be worth while for the public to examine carefully the foundations of this much boasted philosophy.

At the risk of revealing our weakness in argument, we propose three statements concerning evolution. First, The Theory is Unscientific; second, the Theory is Unscriptural; third, the Theory is Anti-Christian.

## THE THEORY IS UNSCIENTIFIC

*It is suggestion, not a science.* The prevailing opinion that evolution is a modern scientific discovery is false alike to history and to the proper employment of speech. On the authority of Wallace, Lucretius, who lived a hundred years before Christ, in his great poem on "The Nature of Things" expressed the major part of the present-day theory. He held to the molecular belief, that the molecules did not come into actual contact; defined atoms, thought that they were eternal; while admitting the existence of gods, he refused them any share in the construction of the universe, maintaining that it had come by chance, after infinite time, by random motions and collisions, and he tried to account for the introduction of sensation into atoms. He maintained that earth worms came by spontaneous generation, and that in some remote period of the world's history, when heat and moisture abounded, the earth was filled with wombs, out of which were born living things, and after the custom of many a present-day biologist, he contended that the very ground had given existence alike to the lowest forms of life, to every beast and to man.

To be sure, the modern apostles of this faith—Huxley, Darwin, Spencer, Wallace and others, have found for it more attractive phrases, argued it on the ground of likelihood, progression and analogy; but not one of these ever called it a science. They regarded it a theory, and a new theory.

It is not unusual for the smaller followers of great minds to far exceed their masters. The leading evolutionists of the world today do not speak of it as a "science"; they retain the old term of Huxley, Darwin, and Spencer—"theory." But many a preacher who is neither a specialist in Natural History nor in Supernatural Revelation, finds himself involved in what he regards "the conflict between science and theology" and attempts the reconciliation. Since the path by which Science has traveled is strewn with the decaying structures of discarded theories, why should not Andrew White have withheld his endeavor until specialists in biology, geology and paleontology are themselves convinced that evolution is something more than a theory?

Several times in recent years we have questioned fairly competent exponents of this theory as to whether they regarded it a "science," to be answered in almost every instance, "Well, it is generally adopted, the world over, as a working theory for scientific investigation." Now the Standard Dictionary defines "theory" after this manner—"A plan, or scheme subsisting in the mind, but based on principles variable by observation; loosely and popularly, were hypothesis or speculation; hence an individual view." "Science," on the contrary, it describes as "Knowledge gained and verified by exact observation and correct thinking." A theory may be scientific; but to make it such one must produce its verification by exact observation or experiment, whereupon it is no longer a theory. Neither Darwin, Huxley, nor Spencer ever maintained that they had produced such verification of evolution!

But we go a step farther. *The theory of evolution is unproven and unprovable.* Notwithstanding Darwin's "Origin of Species," in the form of a book, the occurrence of a new species, either by natural selection or human cultivation, is unknown. By cultivation man has made the rose more splendid in size, more beautiful and variegated in color, and not a few of the flowers he has even doubled; but no man has yet produced a rose from the seed of sunflower, nor from the pink, nor from anything else than a rose; or even been able to make a grain of rye, similar as it is to the form of other cereals, bring forth oats or wheat, or else than rye. A line from Genesis is the law of natural history, "Every seed after its own kind." The scientists of the world have wrought assiduously to disprove this statement of Holy Scripture; but their endeavors to overthrow the Divine fiat have signally failed.

When a biologist who believes that all life, from an amoeba to a Milton, is the product of evolution, being asked if such a thing as a new species, by natural selection is known, answers, "We think there are some snails in the Hawaiian

Islands that hint at it," he will not blame us if we regard his investigations a little "slow." Or, if he affirms that the gill slits of a human foetus prove that man has ascended from sea life, we answer, "That sounds fishy." If he point to the mule in defense of his doctrines, we remind him of its sterility, and make his argument asinine. Not a few scientists have said, concerning the mule, that with his accustomed stubbornness he "blocks the way of the evolution theory." But better still is the remark of Dr. A. J. Frost that "the mule is the endeavor of an ass to evolute himself, but he only succeeds in making a bigger ass of himself."

The utter desperation to which evolutionists are driven in their desire to "demonstrate"—as the Christian (?) Scientist (?) says—and so be able to switch from theory to science, is shown in their treatment of the horse. They have dug out of the earth a little animal about the size of a fox, with five toes, which has some similarity to the horse, and they have called him—old horse-eohippus; and they have brought up another with three toes, as big as a timber wolf, and because of certain similarities they have called him a horse; and then they have imagined that horse finally developing into the present beautiful beast of domestic service, with one toe elongated from the knee to the hoof; and in certain splints on the side of his leg they find the aborted toes. The intervening horses, bridging the gap between these ancient animals and our black beauty, they have sought in vain! Yet they will stand before you and speak with all the assurance of men who had found the last missing link, concerning the evolution of the horse! Why do they begin with that little fox-like animal? In the ocean there is a shrimp that has the head of a horse and his motions in water are much like a plunging charger. Why not begin with him? At college the boys used to be chargeable with having ridden a pony, and if it could be proven it was worse for them when they came into the professor's presence. Once a cute lad, who was later a consul in one of the South American Republics, bluntly remarked in the presence of our professor, "I had a pony last season that thirteen rode; but I gave him away because this present class has nineteen big fellows in it, and I thought it would be an outrage for us all to straddle the little fellow!" But that poor pony of the five toes has been straddled by a thousand professors; they have ridden the toes off him, and it is little wonder that some of their students have gone out to pity the pony and regard the professors' conduct with ridicule.

Something similar has occurred in the attempt to make a man out of a monkey. They found the missing link once in "The Calaveras Skull." It was 150 feet below surface. There could be no doubt about it! But when Wm. R. C. Scribner confessed that he had brought it into the mine as a practical joke, scientists were ashamed. Dr. W. J. Sinclair's discussion, "Recent Investigations Bearing on the Question of the Occurrence of Neocene Man in the Auriferous Gravels of the Sierra Nevada" confirms Scribner's claim, and makes it perfectly evident that Prof. J. D. Whitney paraded a very modern skull as that of a prehistoric man.

They found the missing link in the Neanderthal skeleton in Prussia, and proclaimed it three hundred thousand years old; but it turned out to be only a Cossack killed in 1814. Columbia College had a smart professor who dug out of Colorado's soil a skeleton. It was heralded as of remarkable antiquity, and the friable bones were being paraded to the ends of the earth when some cowboys complained that the grave of their pet monkey had been rifled. To be sure, the greatest ado has been made over the Pithecanthropus Erectus. It consists of the piece of a skull and leg bone and two teeth, found in Java, in 1891. Dr. Alexander Patterson says the cubic measurement of that skull is sixty inches—the same as that of an idiot. These specimens were found at separate places and times. The skull is too small for the thigh bone. The age of the strata in which they were found is uncertain. Even Haeckel admits that the belief that this is the missing link is strongly combated by some distinguished scientists.

The earth has been opened at a thousand points; the sea has been explored to its bottom; biologists have had access to the very bowels of both and have been animated by one determination—the discovery of the missing link—and yet to the present hour they have utterly failed to produce it! We fear that it is an illustration of what the Irishman said. He attended the circus and was especially interested in the dromedary. He examined the ungainly beast from head to foot; felt of the great humps to see whether they were artificial or actual flesh. Being convinced of the latter, he said, "Begory, they ain't no sich animal!"

This seems to be the truth concerning the missing link. It is one thing to imagine that it exists; it is another to make the demonstrations, and science demands the latter.

*Its conclusions are without premises.* What evidence is there that the universe began in fire-mist? What evidence is there that life originated out of death? What evidence is there that mineral became the vegetable, and vegetable became the animal, and the animal became the man? What proof have we of the eternity of matter beyond the atheistic desire to have it so? And if these premises are false, how can conclusions resting upon them be true. If within the knowledge of man the reptile has never become a bird, a fish has never become a mammal, a monkey has never become a man; if the depths of the earth and the sounding of the seas refuse to deliver up a single instance of such a metamorphosis, what are the premises of this argument?

It may be very convenient to push claims back to the time where the knowledge of man utterly fails, but do not do violence to the splendid attainments of human speech by calling such conduct "scientific." I may have no right to object to Mr. Darwin's believing that "man is descended from a hairy quadruped, furnished with a tail, and pointed ears; probably arboreal in its habits, and an inhabitant of the Old World," but I can not be denied the right to ask him to produce some evidence of his assertion. Dr. Eldridge, of the British Museum, declares that that institution is filled with specimens, every one of which disproves the evolution theory. Dr.

12

Joseph Clark, after spending twenty-nine years in the heart of Africa, said: "I find no evidence of evolution in Africa, but positive proofs to the contrary."

*The greatest Scientists are now saying the theory is unscientific.* The reading of Prof. L. T. Townsend's "Collapse of Evolution" brings abundant proof of this assertion. This statement applies not only to the Darwinian theory of Evolution, but equally to all the improved and patented types of this general hypothesis.

Dr. N. S. Shaler, Professor of Geology in Harvard, is quoted: "It begins to be evident to Naturalists that the Darwinian hypothesis is still essentially unverified. . . . It is not yet proved that a single species of the two or three millions now inhabiting the earth, had been established solely or mainly by the operation of Natural Selection."

Professor C. C. Everett, also of Harvard, speaking of evolution, says: "If, in the past, those ranks of beings ever rose and moved in procession along the upward slope, each passing, by no matter how slow a step, out of its own limitations, and in itself, or in its posterity entered upon a larger life, it was before the eyes of man were opened to them. No searching of his awakened powers can detect, even among the remains of an unknown antiquity, any glimpse of the great movement while in progress of accomplishment. All, as he looks upon it, is as fixed as the sphinx, that slumbers on the Egyptian sands. All this story of transformation and activity is a dream."

Professor Lionel S. Beale, physiologist, and professor of anatomy and pathology in King's College, London, in his special field, that of biology, is, with one exception, perhaps, without a peer in any country of the world. While addressing the Victoria Institute of London, he said: "The idea of any relation having been established between the non-living and living, by a gradual advance from lifeless matter to the lowest forms of life and so onwards to the higher and more complex, has not the slightest evidence from the facts of any section of living nature of which anything is known."

Prof. Virchow of Berlin, the greatest German authority in physiology, and "the foremost chemist on the globe," at one time a pronounced advocate of Darwin's and Haeckel's views, subsequently, in his famous lecture on "Freedom of Science," while speaking of evolution, made this statement: "It is all nonsense. It cannot be proved by science that man descends from the ape or from any other animal. Since the announcement of the theory, all real scientific knowledge has proceeded in the opposite direction."

In a recent number of *Beweis des glaubens*, Professor Zoeckler, of the University of Greifswald, employs these words: "The claim that the hypothesis of descent is secured scientifically must most decidedly be denied."

Professor Fleischmann, of Erlangen, one of the several recent converts to anti-Darwinism, in a book published in Leipsic, "Die Darwin's che Theorie," reaches this conclusion: "The Darwinian theory of descent has in the realms of nature not a single fact to confirm it. It is not the result of scientific research, but purely the product of the imagination."

The most suggestive words, however, and really the severest criticism on evolution, though not spoken with that intent, are from Professor Ernst Haeckel, of Jena, Germany's greatest biologist, and the rankest naturalistic evolutionist of recent date. In his latest utterances he bewails the fact that he is standing almost alone. "Most modern investigators of science have come to the conclusion," he says, "that the doctrine of evolution and particularly Darwinism is an error and cannot be maintained." Then he enumerates several distinguished men, whom he calls "bold and talented scientists," who, not long since were advocates of evolution, but who lately have abandoned it. The men he mentions are Dr. E. Dennert, author of *Vom Sterbelalager des Darwinismus* (1903); Dr. Goette, the Strasburg professor, Prof. Edward Hoppe, known as "the Hamburg Savant," who in his recent pamphlets takes a pronounced position, in the name of religion, against naturalistic evolution; Professor Paulson, of Berlin, who, among his other criticisms of evolution, has recently declared that Haeckel's theory "is a disgrace to the philosophy of Germany"; Professor Rutemeyer, geologist and paleontologist, of Basel, who charges evolutiontists, especially of the Haeckel type, with "playing false with the public, and with the natural sciences,' and Professor Wilhelm Max Wundt, of Leipsic.

15

The amazing thing, is, as Professor Townsend remarks, the utter dishonesty of those American professors , and ignorance of those American Preachers, who, on occasion, and oft, without occasion, assure audiences that all great Scientists are evolutionists.

Such speakers have come to use the term "Science" almost as loosely as the followers of Mary Baker Eddy do!

## THE THEORY IS UNSCRIPTURAL

*The Word nowhere warrants it.* There are brethren in the pulpit who have a new way of interpreting the first chapter of Genesis, which, by the way, one of my fellow-laborers has translated after the following manner:

1. Primarily the unknowable moved upon cosmos and evolved protoplasm.

2. And, protoplasm was inorganic and undifferentiated; containing all things in potential energy; and a spirit of evolution moved upon the fluid mass.

3. And the Unknowable said, Let atoms attract; and their contact begat light, heat and electricity.

4. And the Unconditioned differentiated the atoms each after its kind; and their combination begat rock, air and water.

5. And there went out a spirit of Evolution from the Unconditioned, and working in protoplasm by accretion and absorption produced the organic cell.

16

6. And cell by nutrition evolved primordial germ, and germ developed protogene; and protogene begat eozoon, and eozoon begat monad, and monad begat animalculae.

7. And animalculae begat ephemra; then began creeping things to multiply on the face of the earth.

8. And earthly atom in protoplasm begat molecule, and thence came grass and every herb of the earth.

9. And animalculae in the water evolved fins, tails, claws and scales; and in the air wings and beaks; and on the land they sprouted such organs as were necessary as played upon by the environment.

10. And by accretion and absorption, came the radiata and mollusca, and mullusca begat articulata, and articultata begat vertebrate.

11. Now these are the generations of the higher vertebrata in the cosmic period that the Unknowable evolved the biped mammalia:

12. And every man of the earth, while he was yet a monkey, and the horse, while he was yet the hipparion, and the hipparion before he was an oredon. Out of the ascidian came the amphibian and begat the pentadactyle, and by inheritance and selection, produced the hylobate, from which are the simiade in all their tribes.

13. And out of the simiade the lemur prevailed above his fellow and produced the platyrhine monkey.

17

*49*

14. And the polatyrhine begat the catarrhine, and the catarrhine begat the anthropoid ape and the ape begat the longimanous orang, and the orang begat the chimpanzee, and the chimpanzee evolved the what-is-it?

15. And the what-is-it? went into the land of Nod, and took him a wife of the longimanous gibbons.

16. And in the process of the cosmic period were born unto them their children the anthromorphic premordial types.

17. The homunculus, the prognathus; the troglodyte, and the autochthon, the terragon,—these are the generations of primeval man.

13. And primeval man was naked and not ashamed, but lived in quadrumanous innocence, and struggled mightily to harmonize with the environment.

19. And by inheritance and natural selection did he progress from the stable and homogeneous to the complex and the heterogeneous; for the weakest died, and the strongest grew and multiplied.

20. And man grew a thumb for that he had need of, and developed capacities for prey.

21. For behold, the swiftest animals got away from the slow men, wherefore the slow animals were eaten and the slow men starved to death.

22. And as the types differentiated the weaker types continually disappeared.

23. And the earth was filled with violence; for man strove with man, and tribe with tribe, whereby they killed off the weak and foolish and secured "the survival of the fittest."

Moses again appeals to the public, "Choose you this day which you will have"—what the Spirit saith, or what the self-styled Scientist asserteth!

*At many points evolution is anti-scriptural.* The majority of evolutionists, certainly the most able ones among them, contend for the eternity of matter. The Scriptures assert the opposite. "By faith we understand that the worlds have been framed by the Word of God; so that which is seen hath not been made out of things which appeared." (Heb. 11:3.)

Almost to a man, evolutionists contend that species are the product of natural selection. Ten times in the first chapter of Genesis the law "after its own kind" is declared, and it covers every form of life, from the blade of grass to the god-like occupants of Eden. It is little wonder, therefore, that when such men as Crawford H. Toy, George Burman Foster, B. Fay Mills, Charles Aked and R. J. Campbell adopt the evolution theory *in toto*, they immediately begin to treat the Word of God as though it were without authority. And it is hardly to be wondered at that Prof. Haeckel, the most noted evolutionist, should proceed, in his "Riddles of the Universe" to read God out of it altogether. However, there is one thing to be said in favor of these men. They are intelligent enough to see the inharmony between the Scriptures and this present-day popular theory; and honest enough to say, "We prefer evolution to the Book." It is easier to hold such men in esteem than it is to respect those who go up and down the land telling us that evolution is true, and so is the Bible. Such teachers seem to belong with the boy Dr. John Henry Barrows is reported to have met in India. "A native lad had attended the Christian schools and learned there the shape and situation of the earth, but in his Hindoo home he had been taught the Hindoo cosmogony, namely, that the earth was circled by salt water, and that by a circle of earth, and these by successive circles of sweet cane juice and other soft drinks, with intervening circles of land. Dr. Barrows asked the boy which belief he would hereafter hold. He replied that he would believe both.

## THE THEORY AND FALSE THEOLOGY

The intimate relation between this theory and theology is becoming more and more apparent. It is doubtful if there is a single skeptical professor or preacher in the Old World or the New, who is not also a fairly full-fledged evolutionist. The theological result is perfectly evident in such books as "The Finality of the Christian Religion" and the "New Theology."

According to evolutionists, *God is a force*, and those ministers who have accepted the evolutionary theory of the natural universe, have lost their personal heavenly Father in consequence. The shibboleth of such professed Christian preachers is one with that of the atheistic philosophers when they have found a common viewpoint in evolution. It is a remarkable fact to find Daniel, when he comes to describe the coming Prince who shall oppose God, and magnify himself beyond all, literally saying, "But in his estate he shall honor the god of force." (Dan. 11:38.) Are our Critics the forerunners of the anti-Christ?

*Evolution makes Christ only a remarkable man.* One calls Him "the only man"; another believes that He was the "mental product of excessive admiration." "The Flower of the Race" is so beautiful an expression, that quite a few of them agree in its adoption. But, whatever the expression, essential deity is never intended, and to admit that He was begotten by the Holy Ghost would introduce supernaturalism, which they repudiate. Prof. Foster's astonishment that "belief in the virgin birth of Jesus should ever have been held as a cardinal article of the Christian faith" is shared by a majority of the Darwinians.

*Christ's resurrection from the dead* is either denied outright or else explained away by affirming that it was not physical. His promise to come again at the end of the Age and introduce a milennium wherein He himself shall "reign from sea to sea and from the rivers to the ends of the earth" they repudiate to a man, and so fulfill the prediction of Peter, "In the last days mockers shall come, walking after their own lusts and saying, Where is the promise of his coming; for from the day that the fathers fell asleep all things continue as they were from the beginning of creation."

21

*This theory makes sin essentially a virtue.* Man is not a fallen creature. One of their best exponents, a good representative of a great university, recently affirmed that "to tell children they were not 'by nature' children of God, was irrational; to instruct them that the essential thing was the evolution of the life within them, was sanity." To such teachers "sin" is not "a transgression of the law of God," but simply false strokes in the struggle to be free from self-limitations and opposing environments. While compelled to admit that a crab-apple will never produce pippins unless the latter be grafted in, they yet insist that the child, which the Scripture declares is "conceived in sin and shapen in iniquity," can become a saint without "the grafting in" of the new nature, or the regenerating work of the Holy Ghost. To them, Paul's description of sin as "exceedingly sinful" is without justification, and the prophet's statement, "The soul that sinneth it shall die" should be changed to "The soul that sinneth is searching after life."

To be sure some of the greater minds among them do not go to these lengths. Henry Drummond held to the necessity of the new birth, but for that matter, Drummond's "Natural Law in the Spiritual World" is the very antithesis of the full fledged evolution theory.

*The resurrection is even more offensive* to evolutionists, than is regeneration. It just as certainly introduces the supernatural, and it brings the work of the Spirit before the natural vision where men can see and judge for themselves His appearance to "above five hundred brethren at once" (1 Cor. 15:6) is boldly disputed, and the explanation of their testimony is found in the fervor with which these deluded disciples loved their leader.

*It makes the cross only a criminal mistake.* From their viewpoint it was not according to prophecy, nor did it in any wise profit the race. It was only a notable one among the many instances where men, actuated by human hatred and selfishness, have ignorantly slain their friend. As a rule, they scoff the notion that "He bore our sins on the tree," and will have none of the teaching that "by the shedding of His blood" we have secured our "remission." Christ crucified, is unto these, as to the Jews of old, "a stumbling block," and as unto the Gentiles of former times, "foolishness."

*To them redemption is a misleading term.* The thought of God's buying back, with His precious blood, that which man had forfeited to the Adversary is little better than a jest. "Salvation must be by self-development" they insist! Paul, when he dares to say, "By grace are ye saved, through faith, and that not of yourselves," is simply mistaken.

What then, is the conclusion of the whole matter? Some writer has summed it up after this manner: "A pantheistic god, instead of a personal God. A human Saviour instead of a divine Saviour. Infallible scholarship instead of an infallible Bible. Reformation instead of regeneration. Culture instead of conversion. The natural in all things, the supernatural in nothing." These are the results of modern scholarship! Certainly, as Dr. A. H. Strong, Ex-President of Rochester Seminary says, "We need a new vision of the Saviour to convince us that Jesus is lifted above space and time, that His existence antedated creation, that He conducted the march of Hebrew history, that He was born of a virgin, suffered on the cross, rose from the dead, and now lives forever more, the Lord of the universe, the only God with whom we have to do, our Saviour here and our Judge hereafter. Without a revival of this faith our churches become secularized; mission enterprises will die out and the candlestick will be removed out of its place, as it was in the seven churches of Asia, and as it has been with the apostate churches of New England."

# DARWIN'S PHILOSOPHY AND THE FLOOD

By W. B. Riley

TEN CENTS PER COPY

# W. B. RILEY'S FORTY VOLUMES

## The Bible of the Expositor and the Evangelist

*Representing Thirty Years of Labor*

*Twenty-six Volumes Already Off the Press*

Cloth binding (Mailing 15 cents extra) ..................................$1.00
Paper binding (Mailing 10 cents extra) ..................................... .50

**Other Books by the Same Author**
*Larger Works*

Revival Sermons .......................$1.50
Evolution of the Kingdom, paper (A full discussion of the Second Coming) ..................... .75
Inspiration or Evolution, paper 75c, cloth ............................ 1.25
Perennial Revival, cloth............ 1.25
Crisis of the Church, cloth........ 1.25
The Blight of Unitarianism (New) a series of five sermons. (postpaid) ................. .50
God Hath Spoken...................... 1.75
   (500 pages of addresses by the leading Bible expositors of the world. A text book on the Christian Fundamentals.)

# Darwin's Philosophy and the Flood

### By W. B. Riley

*And the* LORD *said unto Noah, Come thou and all thy house into the ark; for thee have I seen righteous before me in this generation.*

*2. Of every clean beast thou shalt take to thee by sevens, the male and his female; and of beasts that are not clean by two, the male and his female.*

*3. Of fowls also of the air by sevens, the male and the female; to keep seed alive upon the face of all the earth.*

*4. For yet seven days, and I will cause it to rain upon the earth forty days and forty nights; and every living substance that I have made will I destroy from off the face of the earth.*

*5. And Noah did according unto all that the* LORD *commanded him.*

*6. And Noah was six hundred years old when the flood of waters was upon the earth.*

*7. And Noah went in, and his sons, and his wife, and his sons' wives, with him, into the ark, because of the waters of the flood.*

8. *Of clean beasts, and of beasts that are not clean, and of fowls, and of every thing that creepeth upon the earth.*

9. *There went in two and two unto Noah into the ark, the male and the female, as God had commanded Noah.*

10. *And it came to pass, after seven days, that the waters of the flood were upon the earth.*

11. *In the six hundredth year of Noah's life, in the second month, the seventeenth day of the month, the same day were all the fountains of the great deep broken up, and the windows of heaven were opened.*

12. *And the rain was upon the earth forty days and forty nights.*

13. *In the selfsame day entered Noah, and Shem, and Ham, and Japheth, the sons of Noah, and Noah's wife, and the three wives of his sons with them, into the ark;*

14. *They, and every beast after his kind, and all the cattle after their kind, and every creeping thing that creepeth upon the earth after his kind, and every fowl after his kind, every bird of every sort.*

15. *And they went in unto Noah into*

[ 4 ]

the ark, two and two of all flesh, wherein is the breath of life.

16. And they that went in, went in male and female of all flesh, as God had commanded him: and the LORD shut him in.

17. And the flood was forty days upon the earth; and the waters increased, and bare up the ark, and it was lift up above the earth.

18. And the waters prevailed, and were increased greatly upon the earth; and the ark went upon the face of the waters.

19. And the waters prevailed exceedingly upon the earth; and all the high hills, that were under the whole heaven, were covered.

20. Fifteen cubits upward did the waters prevail; and the mountains were covered.

21. And all flesh died that moved upon the earth, both of fowl, and of cattle, and of beast, and of every creeping thing that creepeth upon the earth, and every man;

22. All in whose nostrils was the breath of life of all that was in the dry land, died.

23. And every living substance was destroyed which was upon the face of the ground, both man, and cattle, and the creeping things, and the fowl of the heaven; and they were destroyed from the earth;

*and Noah only remained alive, and they that were with him in the ark.*

24. *And the waters prevailed upon the earth an hundred and fifty days.*

(GEN. 7: 1-24.)

"*And Noah builded an altar unto the* LORD; *and took of every clean beast, and of every clean fowl, and offered burnt-offerings on the altar. And the* LORD *smelled a sweet savour; and the* LORD *said in his heart, I will not again curse the ground any more for man's sake; for the imagination of man's heart is evil from his youth; neither will I smite any more every thing living as I have done. While the earth remaineth, seedtime and harvest, and cold and heat, and summer and winter, and day and night shall not cease.*" (GENESIS 8: 20-22.)

I have spoken to this subject of Evolution many times as my volumes, "The Theory of Evolution and False Theology," "The Menace of Modernism," "The Crisis of the Church," "Inspiration or Evolution," bear testimony.

But as Darwinism is still propagated and defended by many teachers and professors, it becomes necessary to revert to the subject often enough to save youth from its deception and snares.

[ 6 ]

Theologians have been charged with dogmatism; and in fact, theology is dogmatic, if it is worthy of the name, for it means the Word of God, and either that must be dogmatic or it is a misnomer.

However, we are not without company in strength of assertion. La Conte, the famous American professor, who was also an evolutionist, conceded that conservatives in theology were not the only dogmatists. He said, "Many seem to think that theology has a preemptive right to dogmatism. If so, then modern materialistic science has jumped the claim."

Certainly La Conte was justified in his remark. We know of no theologians, schooled or ignorant, who have affirmed the tenets of their faith with more certainty than the devotees of Darwinism declare their convictions. It is altogether customary for them now to say that "evolution is a proven science, and is as well established as the law of gravity."

It shall be our purpose in this discussion to investigate a bit and find out whether this report of the flood can be confirmed as a fact, and if so, whether that fact can be reconciled with the philosophy of Darwin. We have deliberately chosen this Scripture because it brings us straight to a disputed realm, namely, that of geology;

and furthermore, because we feel an absolute confidence that this biblical record can be justified, and in its justification becomes the death knell of the whole Darwin claim.

To the text then.

## *THE BIBLICAL FLOOD*

The record of this 7th chapter, interpreted as it must be, in the light of the chapters that precede and follow the same, is concise and clear. There is no ambiguity about it. Little boys and girls in the Sunday School readily understand the story of the flood and having once heard the same, **never forget it**. This is due not alone to the circumstance that it was a world catastrophe, but just as much to the simple straightforward manner in which the story is told. For men to say that it is a mere myth is to show themselves unschooled.

The flood story finds its complete defense in human history, and wide-spread tradition and is confirmed alike by tell-tale rocks. In other words, geology comes to the defense of Genesis in the whole matter, and its testimony is overwhelming as we shall see when the same is reached. In fact, that testimony is such as finds no explanation apart from the story recorded in the 6th, 7th and 8th chapters of the book of Genesis.

[ 8 ]

Let us turn then to the history both written alike in the books of man and found plainly printed upon the leaves of God's book, the rocky strata of the earth.

THE TRADITIONS TOUCHING THE FLOOD ARE FULL.

This is conceded alike by secular and sacred writings.

The Encyclopaedia Britannica, ninth edition, says, "The deluge is a submersion of the world, related by various nations as having taken place in a primitive age, and in which all, or nearly all, living beings are said to have perished."

Among the Babylonians the flood story took the form of the god Kronos, who appeared to the tenth king of that country, in a dream, and warned him of the coming deluge. The Encyclopaedia says, "The details remind us a good deal of the biblical narrative."

The Jewish narrative is the one now before us for study.

The Britannica continues, "The deluge story exists in several forms in Indian literature."

Of course they refer to the East Indian literature.

"In Greece there appeared to have been several floating flood stories. They all rep-

[ 9 ]

resent the flood destroying all but a few men."

At that point they are in harmony with the biblical record.

Concerning the tradition in America, Catlin says that "amongst 120 different tribes that he has visited in North and South and Central America, not a tribe exists that has not related to him distinct or vague traditions of such a calamity, in which one, or three, or eight persons were saved above the waters on the top of a high mountain."

In passing we call attention to the fact that this slight divergence—"one" or "three" or "eight persons"—is a practical confirmation of Genesis. Noah is the conspicuous person with whom God dealt, and might be regarded as the one of the story; his three sons might be reckoned as the three in another, as the propagating male members of the family were commonly regarded by the ancients; or the whole eight saved in Noah's ark might be reported as in the Biblical—a correct and complete record.

Hugh Miller believes and teaches in the "Testimony of the Rocks" that the deluge story was propagated from a single center, a fact that would also tend to confirm Genesis, for if all the people of the earth

[ 10 ]

perished save Noah and his family, it could not be otherwise.

Turning now to more sacred sources, The International Standard Bible Encyclopaedia has the following to say concerning the flood, "Compared with other traditions of the deluge, the Bible account appears in a most favorable light, while the general prevalence of such traditions strongly confirms the reality of the Bible story."

It has been denied by the Britannica (9th Edition) that Egypt had any such story. On the contrary, the Standard Encyclopaedia says,

"In Egyptian documents themselves we find Raa, the creator, on account of the insolence of man, proceeded to exterminate him by a deluge of blood which flowed up to Heliopolus, the home of the gods. But the heinousness of the deed so affected him that he repented and swore nevermore to destroy mankind.

"The Chinese tradition concerning the flood is narrated after this manner: 'Now the pillars of heaven were broken and the earth shook to its very foundation; the sun and the stars changed their motions; the earth fell to pieces, and the water enclosed within its bosom burst forth with violence and overflowed it. Man having rebelled against heaven, the system of the universe

[ 11 ]

was totally disordered, the grand harmony of nature destroyed. All of these evils arose from man's despising the supreme power of the universe.'"

He who said, therefore, that the flood was as well established a fact of history as was the burning of Moscow or the Reign of Terror in France, was absolutely justified. An open mind can be convinced. Infidelity is impervious to truth!

But we have remarked that there is another history worthy of consultation, namely

THE TELL-TALE FEATURES OF NATURE.

In the November 1930 number of THE CHRISTIAN FUNDAMENTALIST, Prof. D. A. Straw of Wheaton College contributes an article on "A Consistent Cosmology." This is only the first in a series.

In that article he makes suggestions that certainly demand serious consideration. He holds that until the flood, rain had never fallen on the earth but as Genesis 2: 5-6 says,

*"The Lord had not caused it to rain on the earth, but there went up a mist from the earth and watered the whole face of the ground."*

There is indisputable evidence to the effect that the world back of the flood time

[ 12 ]

neither had need of rain, nor atmospheric conditions that would produce it. As one geologist says, "All the fossils give us proof of an almost eternal spring having prevailed in the arctic regions, and semi-tropical conditions in the north temperate latitudes; in short, give us proof of a single uniformity of climate over the globe which we can hardly conceive possible, let alone account for."

Prof. Straw undertakes to account for this climate by reason of the fact that at that time the equator of the earth was in perfect line with its orbit, a condition that would give it a uniformly tropical atmosphere, the sun striking the portions of the same with equal light and warmth, and which would also effect a humid atmosphere such as would produce the most luxuriant growth of vegetation, and also of animal life.

There being no extremes of heat or cold, rain would not be formed, but the mist would rise and fall with the downgoing and up-coming of the sun. He then postulates or supposes that a meteor of enormous size struck the earth, producing the cataclysm, and moving the earth's equator $23\frac{1}{2}$ degrees out of line with its orbit, effecting such an inclination of the ecliptic.

Instantly a number of things would oc-

[ 13 ]

cur found recorded in geological formations.

Cold would come to the shadowed poles of the earth both north and south, freezing them solid in a few hours, encasing forever in frozen form both their animal and vegetable occupants.

The same cold would change that regular and almost unchanging atmosphere into extremes of heat and cold, that would produce not only rain, but such a flood as is recorded in these chapters of Genesis, bringing the ocean that was in the atmosphere, "the waters which were above the firmament," Gen. 1:7, back to the earth again, chilling its vapor into immeasurable waters.

Such an explanation, if true, would clarify many long debated subjects.

First of all, it would account for the flood itself, as well as conform to the statement in Genesis 2:5-6.

In the next place, it would account for those great mastodons and other animals of the north pole region, who were caught by some catastrophe and frozen in so suddenly and securely that their flesh is not decomposed to this day.

In the third place, the tidal and translation waves sweeping the earth around would mingle with the ice of the north and south poles the sands that hold these mastodons in the very embrace of earth itself, cut water channels of rivers, corrode mountains, and pile rock and sand on lower levels thousands of feet deep in a few days.

Still further, it would account for the great coal deposits, for it would cover the enormous vegetation that must have existed upon the earth in such a humid and tropical atmosphere, with mud, stone and sands; and to such enormous depths as by heat and pressure would convert the same into the great coal deposits that are now found upon the face of the earth.

At the same time it would lay strata after strata over the dead animals and animalculae, that might account not alone for the great quantity of gas and oil now coming out of the bowels of the earth, but for the enormous depth ranging from hundreds of feet to many thousands, at which these substances, that always tend to rise, are found buried.

Furthermore, it is the only explanation of those great bone deposits that characterize the eastern and western shores of North America, and are found in heaps in other portions of the earth. Animals do not die in huddles, nor do they crawl to some graveyard and lay themselves upon the bones of their ancestors to breathe their last, but such a flood as is recorded in Genesis, drowning the animals of the earth, would by the tidal and translation waves thereof, tend to pile them in exactly such ricks, on ocean shore lines, with the final recession of waters to sea beds, as daily investigation is bringing to the light.

The flood also would account for the fact that the Werner Uniformitarian stratification is not uniform, for it would lay down in such layers, as its caprice might accomplish, any condition of rock or sand or coral or other earth material as such a catastrophe could accomplish perfectly in 150 days.

In further proof of the Bible record of the flood, take the testimony of C. Leonard Woolley of the Pennsylvania University:

"We had descended 26 feet in our excavation at Ur of the Chaldees, when one of the workmen reported he had come upon Virgin Soil. I examined the clay, and then ordered the digging to be continued. Eight feet below the surface of this water-laid clay, we found thousands of pieces of inscribed tablets, arrows and painted pottery."

"The 8-foot stratum of clay," says Prof. Woolley, "can have resulted only from a flood of unexpected magnitude"—"the flood of the book of Genesis."

It would wipe from the earth those great

[ 16 ]

Saurians that feasted upon its luxuriant vegetation, and pile them up in heaps of the dead, exactly as the Wyoming excavations discovered them a few years since, burying them in the rock of the plateau, 7,000 feet above the sea level, since their great hulks would not tend to drift away with the receding waves as did those of lesser animal life.

Only recently Harold Cook was reported to have found in Yuma County, Arizona, bones of a huge mammoth that had been hacked with flint knives by the ancient butchers, the knives lying beside the bones, proving that these mammoths lived along with man, and not millions of years before him as has long been contended.

The flood is the solitary explanation of all of these facts, and since it is stated in sacred Scripture, is confirmed by the traditions of every nation, and proven by the face of nature, why refuse to believe, and pay proper tribute to the Book Divine?

## THE DARWIN PHILOSOPHY

We insist upon questioning this philosophy, and in looking into the same we find damaging evidences against it.

First of all, IT RESTS ON A SHIFTING BASE.

It was born in the form of a theory;

[ 17 ]

it has never attained to any other stage; it is a theory still.

The very argument that Mr. Darwin himself used, he frankly confessed himself unable to find, namely, an instance of the transmutation of species. He says, "Why then is not every geological formation and every stratum full of intermediate links? Geology assuredly does not reveal any such finely-graduated organic chain; and this, perhaps, is the most obvious and serious objection which can be urged against the theory. The explanation lies, as I believe, in the extreme imperfection of the geological record."

What an imaginary loop-hole of escape!

If the theory even approached fact, the proofs of the same could be found, not by the thousands but by the tens of thousands and by the millions. The whole face of nature would abound with the same, and species in the process of transformation would be dug up as often as the fixed forms have been found.

Professor James, the great modern philosopher (and evolution is a matter of philosophy and not of science), says, "The plain truth is that the philosophy of evolution is a metaphysical creed, and nothing else. It is a mood of contemplation, an emotional attitude, rather than a system of thought—

[ 18 ]

a mood which is as old as the world, and which no refutation of any one incarnation of it (such as the Spencerian philosophy) will dispel; the mood of fatalistic pantheism, with its intuition of One and All which was, and is, and ever shall be, and from whose womb each single thing proceeds. . . . What we at present call scientific discoveries had nothing to do with bringing it to birth. . . . It can laugh at the phenomenal distinctions on which science is based, for it draws its vital breath from a region which—whether above or below—is at least altogether different from that in which science dwells. A critic, however, who cannot disprove the truth of the metaphysic creed, can at least raise his voice in protest against its disguising itself in 'scientific' plumes."

Again, Mr. Darwin himself says, "The great break in the organic chain between man and his nearest allies, which cannot be bridged over by any extinct or living species, has often been advanced as a grave objection to the belief that man is descended from some lower form; but this objection will not appear of much weight to those who, from general reasons, believe in the general principle of evolution."

In other words, they are not open to conviction! Resting in a baseless philosophy

[ 19 ]

which does not recognize the laws of Science, nor involve the existence of a God or any responsibility to Him, they are therewith content.

THEY ARE NOT EVEN DISTURBED BY ITS INSUFFICIENT PROOFS.

And insufficient they are! The reason why, after seventy successive years of argument, the plain unprejudiced man is not convinced exists in the circumstance that the arguments are not convincing.

Disraeli was undoubtedly one of the most briliant of modern minds. In spite of his Jewish blood, and the enormous prejudices against which he had to fight, he rose to the level of a Gladstone, and was the one man who dared and did dispute his supremacy. Being a Jew and not committed to the Christian faith, we would expect him to capitulate to this philosophy as the atheistic Jew of the present day so often does. On the contrary, in a notable speech at Oxford, Disraeli said,

"The question is this: 'Is man an ape or an angel?' I am on the side of the angels. I repudiate with indignation and abhorrence the contrary view which is, I believe, foreign to the conscience of humanity. More than that, even in the strictest intellectual point of view, I believe the severest metaphysical analysis is opposed to

[ 20 ]

such a conclusion; but, on the other hand, what does the church teach us—what is the interpretation of the highest nature? It teaches us that man as man is made in the image of his Creator—a source of inspiration and of solace, a source from which only can flow out every right principle of moral and every divine truth. It is between these two contending interpretations of the nature of man and their consequences that society will have to decide. Their rivalry is at the bottom of human affairs. Upon our acceptance of that divine interpretation, for which we are indebted to the Bible and of which the church is the guardian, all sound and salutary legislation depends."

Furthermore, DARWINISM HAS BEEN SHOWN MATHEMATICALLY INCORRECT.

Dr. William A. Williams, ex-President of Franklin College, Ohio, has a volume entitled, "The Evolution of Man Mathematically Disproved," in the introduction to which he says,

"Let it be understood, at the outset, that every proved theory or science is to be accepted. Only the most intense prejudice and the maddest folly would lead any one to reject the proved conclusions of science."

And then he adds,

"If evolution cannot stand the acid test

[ 21 ]

of mathematics, it will be repudiated by all."

And here is the acid test to which he himself subjects it. He says, "The present population of the globe proves that mankind must have descended from one pair who lived not earlier than the time of Noah," and his argument is the Berlin census of 1922 when the population was found to be 1,804,187,000. "If we start with a single pair the race must double itself 30 and 75/100 times to make this number. Beginning with the first period of doubling there would be two human beings; the second, 4, the third, 8; the fourth, 16; the tenth, 1024; the twentieth, 1,048,576; the thirtieth, 1,073,741,824, and the thirty-first, 2,147,483,648."

Therefore it is evident, even to the school boy, that to have the present population of the globe the net population must be doubled more than thirty times and less than thirty-one times, or exactly 30 and 75/100; which is the present population of the globe, and positive confirmation of the whole Noah story.

If man had been on the earth for a million years the population would be non-computable; or if he had been on the earth for even ten thousand years the population would be over two million times as great

[ 22 ]

as it is now, and could not possibly exist upon the globe.

Or, to take the negative form of it. If man has been on the earth two million years the present population only requires that he double his numbers once in 65,040 years; and if that were true, since Abraham's time there would only be found on the earth two and a fraction Jews, instead of the 25,000,000 that exist. Or, if man had been on earth 100,000 years, 3,252 years would be required to double the population, and at that rate, there would be about five Jews on the earth instead of the 25,000,000 there found.

But, as a matter of fact, these gentlemen who boast themselves scientific are not interested in science; they console themselves solely with speculation, and are impervious to proof; and Williams' contention, the population of the earth mathematically proves the flood story, is nothing to them.

In the interbreeding of the races there is demonstrated the creative act of God, and the law that follows, to produce "after their kind."

The languages of the races require no more than seven thousand years for their development, and the religions of the races all find easy explanation within that same

[ 23 ]

period; while the so-called civilizations with their actual history, contain never a hint of prehistoric man.

No wonder Prof. J. Arthur Thompson of Aberdeen, an evolutionist, says: "Modern research is leading us away from the picture of primitive man as brutish, dull, lascivious and bellicose. There is more justification for regarding primitive man as clever, kindly, adventurous and inventive."

In other words, he was a work of God.

But enough! Follow Noah now in the next step

## THE DIVINE FAVOR

The flood was no sooner finished and he, with his family, on firm ground, than he *"built an altar unto the Lord; and took of every clean beast, and of every clean fowl, and offered burnt-offerings on the altar. And the* Lord *smelled a sweet savour; and the* Lord *said in his heart, I will not again curse the ground any more for man's sake; for the imagination of man's heart is evil from his youth; neither will I again smite any more every thing living, as I have done. While the earth remaineth, seedtime and harvest, and cold and heat, and summer and winter, and day and night shall not cease."* (Gen. 8: 20-22.)

Three suggestions and I close!

GOD WAS KNOWN AND ACKNOWLEDGED BY NOAH.

The man to whom God had given His revelation of the coming flood, whose preservation had been in the form of the divine prescription and salvation of the ark, who had seen the prophecy of the Lord fulfilled to the last letter, was not an atheist.

It is little wonder that not a few men who have been among the foremost of scientists have turned from materialism to faith in a personal God. Haeckel complained of this and named as among his contemporaries, Wundt, Dubois - Reynolds, Virchow and Baer, who had quit materialism for theism.

Haeckel, in his infidelity, attributed this change to a gradual weakening of the brain, but is reported himself to have submitted to the same before his death, just as Lady Hope reported Darwin's repentance.

The fact is that as men come near God it is more difficult to deny God. When Daniel Webster was asked to tell the greatest thought that ever occupied his mind, he answered, "The fact of my personal accountability to God."

We are told that when George III acceded to the throne of England he issued a restraining order to any clergyman who might preach before him, from paying him

[ 25 ]

personal compliment. This command resulted from a fulsome adulation which one Dr. Thomas Wilson indulged in, only to be reprimanded by his Majesty, who said, "I come to this chapel to hear the praises of God and not the praise of self."

If there is one thing this generation needs more than another it is to copy the example of Noah and acknowledge God.

But such an acknowledgment will lead, as it did with Noah, to recognition of sin.

SIN WAS FELT AND SINCERELY CONFESSED.

When he took of *"every clean beast, and every clean fowl, and offered burnt-offerings on the altar"* he was acknowledging his sin. The shedding of blood never had another significance in the Old Testament than an atonement for sin.

Henry Van Dyke, in his "The Gospel for an Age of Doubt," quotes Paul Desjardins as saying, "Never, I believe, have men been more universally sad than in the present time."

And then he adds, "Our misery lies in feeling that we are less men than we were sixty years ago."

He also quotes Stendahl as having said, "I am come, in this series of psychological studies, to the fifth and last of the personages whom I propose to analyze. I have ex-

[ 26 ]

amined a poet, Baudelaire; a historian, Renan; a romancer, Flaubert; a philosopher, Taine; I have just examined one of these composite artists in whom the critic and the imaginative writer are closely united; and I have found in these five Frenchmen of such importance, the same philosophy of disgust with the universal nothingness."

What was the matter with these men? They neither acknowledged God nor sin.

Clifford followed them and said, "God, the Great Companion, is dead."

Possibly, all of this, as Van Dyke contends, gives meaning to the words of St. Augustine. "God has made us for Himself and unquiet is our heart until it rests in Him."

And the way of that rest is plainly in His Word, *"If we confess our sins, he is faithful and just to forgive us our sins, and to cleanse us from all unrighteousness."*

It was cleansing for which Noah sought in the sacrifices, and it is cleaning of which we stand in need, and without which the race will never be free.

But to enjoy the same we must see and understand the significance of this offering.

These clean beasts and birds were types of Christ offered for us on Calvary's cross. Noah was not trusting the blood of bulls or turtle doves; but with their sacrifice was

[ 27 ]

reminding himself of the Lamb slain from the foundation of the world, in whom alone is human hope.

God, then, arranges and accepts sacrifice!

The language of the Book is, *"The Lord smelled a sweet savour: and the Lord said in his heart, I will not again curse the ground any more for man's sake; for the imagination of man's heart is evil from his youth; neither will I again smite any more every thing living, as I have done. While the earth remaineth, seedtime and harvest, and cold and heat, and summer and winter, and day and night shall not cease."*

In other words, "My grace shall be continuous." Oh, how marvelous! It is all of grace!

The story is told that a working man in England was having serious trouble with his eyes. On consulting a famous physician he was informed that there were two cataracts growing over them, and that the only way would be to remove them; and told him to see Dr.——— at once and added, "Do not forget to take plenty of money for his fee is heavy." The working man had 20 pounds in the bank. He drew it out and went to see the great doctor. On examination, the specialist said, "Your physician

[ 28 ]

has diagnosed your case correctly. I can cure you but it will cost you one hundred guineas."

"Then," said the working man, "I will have to go blind for I have but twenty pounds."

The specialist replied, "You cannot come up to my terms, nor can I come down to yours; but there is another way open, I will perform the operation gratis."

That is the sinner's ground of hope.

*"Amazing grace, how sweet the sound,*
 *That saved a wretch like me!*
*I once was lost, but now am found,*
 *Was blind, but now I see.*

*" 'Twas grace that taught my heart to fear,*
 *And grace my fears relieved;*
*How precious did that grace appear*
 *The hour I first believed!*

*"Thro' many dangers, toils and snares,*
 *I have already come;*
*'Tis grace hath brot me safe thus far,*
 *And grace will lead me home.*

*"When we've been there ten thousand years.*
 *Bright shining as the sun,*
*We've no less days to sing God's praise*
 *Than when we first begun."*

## 10c Booklets

The Church After 1900 Years
The Challenge of Orthodoxy
Bryan, the Great Commoner and Christian
Christ and His City
Will Christ Come Again?
Shall We Longer Tolerate the Teaching of Evolution?
The Eclipse of Faith
Fundamentalism—What Is It?
The Scientific Accuracy of the Sacred Scriptures
The Interchurch, or the Kingdom by Violence
Redemption of the Downtown
Theological Liberty vs. License of Infidelity
Socialism in Our Schools
Is Society Rotting?
Civilization—It is an Evolution?
Humanism—Is it Heathenism?
Daniel, or the Doom of Democracy

*All 17 Booklets to One Order,* $1.00

### Order from
## L. W. CAMP
1020 Harmon Place
Minneapolis, Minnesota

# Evolution —
# A FALSE PHILOSOPHY

By W. B. Riley

# Evolution—A False Philosophy

*By* W. B. RILEY, A.M., L.L.D.

*"Then said the prophet Jeremiah unto Hananiah the prophet; Hear now, Hananiah; the Lord hath not sent thee; but thou makest this people to trust in a lie. Therefore thus saith the Lord; Behold I will cast thee from off the face of the earth: this year thou shalt die, because thou hast taught rebellion against the Lord."*—JER. 28:15-16.

*(This sermon was one in a series on the subject)*

In speaking to you on the subject of "Evolution and False Philosophy," I propose the justifying of my subject by the method of making the friends of the theory of Evolution confirm all that I say.

It is quite the custom nowadays for those pseudo-scientists who teach this philosophy to tell the new, uninstructed student that "all scientists are agreed" on the subject, and that its last great opponent is long since dead. Unfortunately, the average freshman, and for that matter the average post-graduate, who has never heard from the opponents of the philosophy or read a single book in opposition to the same, swallows this statement as thoughtlessly as young fledglings take into their stomachs whatever the mother drops into the mouth. Many, later in life, repudiate it.

I have selected the text of this evening in order to show three things, namely:

1.—That the prophets of Evolution are false prophets;
2.—That their claims are false pretences;
3.—and That their judgment is foreordained.

### THE PROPHETS ARE FALSE

Hananiah was a false prophet, and Jeremiah dared to face him and charge him with that fact. *"Hear now, Hananiah; the Lord hath not sent thee."*

That is the exact charge that I make against the prophets of Evolution.

*They are false prophets, every one!*

They seek to substitute a pure

4

speculation for science. In that procedure they distort their profession. They are set by their employers to teach the truth; they are salaried with that intent. The public has a right to expect from them the output of truth. On the contrary, they themselves, having been *"turned to believe a lie,"* propagate the same, and, in order to get it accepted, dare to label "scientific,"—a theory confessedly without verification.

The whole doctrine of transmutation which Spencer himself affirmed was the essential,—the *sine-qua-non* of the hypothesis, is unknown to nature's ways. This fact was admitted by Darwin himself. Here is Darwin's language from "The Descent of Man," the 1874 edition:

"It is asking a great deal of intelligent people to believe the theory which is not supported by evidence, just where evidence is most needed. Now these missing links, if there are any, should be more highly developed than the forms lower down in the scale from which they evolved, and therefore more able to continue. Then why not continue, if they ever evolved, while their weaker progenitors, less able to live, continue to this day?"

5

Now listen to Darwin's answer to his own question:

"But this objection will not appear of much *weight* to those who, from general reasons, believe in the general principle of Evolution."

This is the sad thing of the whole Evolutionary propaganda. The lack of evidence in no wise phases its friends and advocates, a circumstance that proves that they have no kinship to true scientists.

*Their plan for success is the imposition of the philosophy upon immature minds.*

The greatest outrage against childhood in America is not being perpetrated by sweat factories, nor even by unfit and oppressive parents; the greatest outrage to American childhood, at this moment, is a mental outrage.

To take little children, in the third grade, and teach them "The Early History of Man," and bring them to believe that the manufactured and imaginary creations of such a book ever had a historic basis, is to wilfully perpetrate a mental derangement.

To adopt as text books in the Public Schools, "The Tree Boys," and "The Cave Men" is to turn blank time into a Tarzan travesty, and to accomplish all of this with little undefended children, or even with College Freshmen, under the pretense of a new interpretation of Christianity, is a hypocritical and conscienceless procedure.

Some years ago Dr. A. W. Slaten was the Head of Religion in a Baptist College. It had been founded and fostered by Fundamentalists; its very Constitution demanded, on the part of every teacher in the School, loyalty to the great essentials of Christianity. Slaten was an Evolutionist. He believed the School presented an opportunity to influence the future for his philosophy. He persuaded himself that the end of bringing his boys and girls to believe in the same, justified the hypocritical and surreptitious method of putting it over; and in that endeavor he was successful, until, by and by, he foolishly wrote a book that brought to the Board of Control exhibits of his true belief, whereupon he was forced from his Professor-ship.

Inside of a week he was a Unitarian pastor, and inside of three months he was debating the existence of God. In other words, when a monthly salary was removed, he voiced his true views for the first time.

Unfortunately for the youth of America, our State schools now justify themselves in a course such as has been charged. With fair reason, it has been charged against the University of Chicago that "The Academic Department convinces the student that he has no mind! and the Theological course, that there is no God."

The only difference is, that, in our State Universities, the departments of Animal Biology, Philosophy, and the study of the English Bible, unite to do the same work that the University of Chicago Theological Department accomplishes, namely, destroy Faith in God.

Now there are people who imagine that a minister of the Gospel, under such circumstances, should take one of two courses: shut his eyes to the facts and close his ears to the philosophies of modern teaching; or, if he see and hear, seal his lips in the interests of quiet and peace.

Old Martin Luther said, "I was born to fight devils. Pardon the boisterousness of my books. It is my business to remove obstruction, to cut down thorns, to fill up the quagmires, and to open and make straight the paths; but if I must have some failing, let me rather speak the truth with too great severity than act the hypocrite and conceal the same."

To that deliverance we say "Amen."

I turn then from these False Prophets to their

### FALSE PRETENCES

*The claim for Evolution that it is a Science is a false pretence.*

Among the old advocates of this theory that claim was never made, except by Hoeckel. He was the most Atheistic, and, in order to provide a basis for his Atheism, he asserted that Evolution was a Science.

Darwin never made such a claim; Huxley never made it; Wallace never made it. The greater scientists do not now make it.

The declaration that Evolution is a demonstrated Science marks its maker as a diminutive man; and the smaller he is the more loudly he proclaims.

Professor Neuman, zoologist of the University of Chicago, a man who falsified the facts concerning the author of the Tennessee anti-evolution law, then refused, upon proofs to the contrary, to apologize, is one of those American Midget Professors, who dare to say that "Evolution is a guess only in the same sense that the law of gravity is a guess," and yet, in the same conjunction, he has to admit in all frankness, "The Evolutionists volunteer the admission that Evolution is not absolutely proven." It is a joke to put in the word "absolutely," in view of the utter poverty of evidence. It is not proven at any point.

Wm. Bateson, the most eminent biologist of the age, himself an Evolutionist, frankly admitted in his Toronto speech,

"The *assumed* appearance of variability is largely ILLUSORY. Of the occurrence of genetic change which might be likely to lead to the production of new species. NO INDICATION HAS BEEN FOUND. THE IMMEDIATE CONSEQUENCE HAS BEEN THAT THE DEVELOPMENT OF THE EVOLUTIONARY THEORY HAS BEEN TACITLY SUSPENDED."

In a letter received from a student of the Minnesota University, I was asked, "Did it ever occur to you that in the process of evolution,

10

these changes we know about, do not happen in an instant?" to which my answer is, The whole question is begged by such a query. No one knows of such changes!

I have already shown you that Darwin himself admitted that we do not know about them.

Now I come to tell you that Bateson, who, doubtless, was quite as well up on this subject as is the student who wrote the question, says concerning the time question in this imaginary process,

"Even time cannot complete that which is not yet commenced."

*These False Prophets Substitute for Fact Fictional Imagination.*

Think of the following statement of a Minnesota student, and ask yourself if there is one known fact involved in it, and yet it is in practical accord with Van Loon's mental meandering:

"Way back in the dawn of life a bit of *naked* protoplasm rose in the warm seas of the earth; let us say God created it out of the substances in the water, and endowed it with life. Now this bit of living matter was neither plant nor animal, but from it arose two lines of develop-

11

ment,—one to become the future plants, the other the animals."

That is quite a statement. What scientific basis has it? The Standard Dictionary definition of Science is, "Knowledge gained and verified by exact observation and correct thinking."

I do not know the age of the lady who wrote me this statement. I have heard of a spinster who prided herself on having read every book that came from the press. Finally, one day, a friend asked her, "Have you read 'Aesop's Fables'?" to which she replied, "Yes, I read them when they first came out." Aesop died 564 B. C. But that spinster's age was infancy *in comparison*. In fact she was still in fœtal form as compared with sister Fern, if Fern made "exact observation" upon "the rise of the protoplasm."

Professor Lewis T. More, Head of the chair of Physics of the University of Cincinnati, in his "Dogma of Evolution," wisely remarks,

"Some day men of Science will learn that hypotheses cannot always be avoided, but that they are to be used only as a confession of ignorance."

12

## *The Proponents of Evolution Are Specialists in Imagination*

Because they want the theory to be true (that God may be shorn of His creative ability and man may be accepted as the supreme creature of the universe) they will adopt the lamest arguments, and seek, with the crutches of imagination, to provide them standing.

It is not my purpose in the lecture of this night to repeat any considerable portion of what I have said on the previous occasions; but in illustration, let me remind you again that there is not anything like the kin-ship in physical form, appearance, comparison of part with part, between the Eohippus and the modern horse than there is between a jackass and a jack rabbit, and yet, because geology marks indefinite space of time between the former, but brings the latter under man's observation, the first is accepted as a fact, and the second is laughed at as a fancy.

Again, take the two most outstanding of the imaginary links between the monkey and the man, namely, *Pithecanthropus Erectus* and *Piltdown,* and consider their history, and tell me if any man, whose mind has a scintilla of the scientific about it, could bring from these, impressive evidence even, for this philosophy.

Since Pithecanthropus has been most paraded, consider the following thoughtful objections to his place in the Hall of the Age of Man—

I—Professor Dubois found four small bits of bones; the cap of a skull, two teeth, and a femur.

II—Two of these were found in 1891, brought from an old river-bed, and the other two, the left thigh bone and a molar tooth, were found months afterwards in the same vicinity.

III—The teeth were 5 feet apart from the skull, and the femur fifty feet away. Does "observation" or "correct thinking" demand, or even approve, the idea that these parts all originally belonged to one person, or one animal?

IV—*Science,* Aug. 17, 1923, Suppl. VIII, says: "Dubois himself now believes that his much-prized fossils are bones of a large ape, rather than a form of ape-man."

V—His second Pithecanthropus Erectus skull (on the discovery of which he declared a race of such missing links), was finally proven to be the knee-cap of an elephant, as he himself admitted, in an embarrassed confession before the Old World Scientists in their Convention at Amsterdam in 1924.

*Now take Piltdown!* The pieces from which this "Dawn man" was imaginatively created were not found together; not even the two pieces of skull, but separated by a distance of several yards.

The pieces were not found at one time, some months intervening between the discovery of the parts.

The skull and the jaw were apparently mis-fits. According to Keith, the skull is that of a woman; the jaw, according to Hrdlicka, is that of an ape. Professor Keith admits that Woodward had difficulty in securing "an approach to symmetry and a correct adjustment of parts." We should think he would!

Professor J. H. McGregor said that he did not believe the jaw and the skull belonged to the same individual, and Professor W. Waterson agreed to that opinion.

But let Lull, the ardent Evolutionist of Yale University, famed also as a paleontologist, state the objections to this exhibit:

15

"First of all it was in a shallow stratum of gravel, less than four feet in thickneess at the point of discovery."

Second—Lull admits that Smith, Woodward, Keith, and McGregor could not agree upon what it represented, or in their estimation of its cranial capacity.

Third—Lull says, "The jaw proved to be a veritable bone of contention. G. S. Miller, Jr., declared that the jaw and skull could not belong to the same individual, or even the same genus."

According to Prof. Lull in "Evolution of Man," the question of time to which these belonged, is in dispute. Whether the jaw and skull belonged to the same individual is in dispute. Whether the teeth were upper or lower was in dispute. The cubic contents of the skull are in dispute.

In fact, the whole thing is a question mark, and yet it is used in text books as a scientific (?) demonstration of the infidel philosophy of Evolution.

Men who can accept such evidences in a Science realm are hard pressed for proofs.

*There is Not a Step in the Entire Philosophy, but is in dispute.*

I do not mean in dispute as between the opponents of Darwinism and its advocates; but I mean in earnest and hot debate among advocates themselves.

Let me illustrate.—In my attack the other night upon the theory of RECAPITULATION, some student from the Minnesota U. put to me the question,

"Do you profess to be a better embryologist than Professor Scammon?"

To which I replied as you will remember, "Certainly not! Professor Scammon has an excellent reputation as an embryologist, so I understand; but a good reputation as an embryologist does not justify calling the arches that are found in the throat region of a human fœtus, gill-slits, when there is neither a gill nor a slit there at any time!"

Now, I return to that subject, and will bring you the opinions and exact words of men whose names are not only well known in Universities to which they belong, but who have world-wide reputation as Scientists.

Professor T. H. Morgan of Columbia University in "Evolution and

17

Adaptation," p. 83, says of the Recapitulation Theory, "This idea is in principle FALSE."

Professor W. B. Scott of Princeton in "Readings in Evolution," p. 173, says, "This fundamental law is nowadays very seriously questioned, and by some authorities, is altogether denied."

Professor Karl Vogt, Geneva, says: "This law, which I long held as well founded, is absolutely and radically false."

Professor Adam Sedgwick, the eminent English embryologist, in "Darwin and Modern Science," p. 174, says:

"But as Huxley has pointed out and as the whole course of paleontological investigation has demonstrated, the extinct forms of life are very similar to those now existing, and there is nothing specially embryonic about them. So that the facts, as we KNOW them, LEND NO FORCE TO THE THEORY OF RECAPITULATION."

Professor Percy E. Davidson, in his volume "The Recapitulation Theory," printed in 1914, says: "From these authoritative statements it appears that the facts of embryonic resemblances fail to support re-

18

capitulation in all three of its main implications."

Professor A. Weber, Geneva University, in the *Scientific American,* Feb., 1921, p. 121, says: "The critical comments of such embryologists as O. Hertwig, Keibel, and Vialleton, indeed, have practically *torn to shreds* the aforementioned fundamental biogenetic law. Its ALMOST UNANIMOUS ABANDONMENT has left considerably at a loss those investigators who sought in the structure of organisms the key to their remote origin, or to their relationships."

One further illustration to show you at another most important point, how, in the teachings of the present, small Professors are at variance with the great authorities.

I speak of *VESTIGIAL REMAINS!*

A few years ago we were somewhat astounded to be told that we had in our human bodies 180 vestigial remains, each and every one of which pointed back to our animal origin!

These vestigial parts were supposed to have functioned in some former animal ancestor, but to have failed in that function in human life

19

for the simple reason that man's more highly developed frame no longer required their function.

I will not attempt to mention all these vestigial remains; to even name the 180 would require the time allotted to this address; but I shall deal with one or two of the most commonly mentioned, and some others of the most important significance.

For instance, the *Appendix*—

This was supposed to be a vestigial remain; of no value now, but a mortal menace instead; and so everybody who had a pain in the side or could dig up the price, had the pesky thing removed. Now the word comes to us that Dr. Howard A. Kelly, of Johns Hopkins University, says of the appendix, "It increases the extent of the intestinal mucous surface for secretion and absorption." This is also the position of Sir Arthur Keith.

Take the Thyroid Glands!

They were supposed to be useless vestigial organs. They are located on either side of the windpipe, just below the larynx. Now we learn that if they are removed from a cat or dog it means death; and if they have been defective in a human mother it will produce cretinism. Dr. C. W. Saleeby says of the thyroid that "it creates a unique substance, mostly consisting of iodine. Without it, none can live."

Take the *Pituitary Body!*

It was called another vestigial remain. Vincent says, "It was established by Paulesco in 1906, that the organ is essential for life. When removed from animals the operation is fatal." It helps to regulate secretions from various glands of the body, and its failure to function properly will produce giantism,—or it may result in the opposite,—infantilism.

Take the *Pineal Body!*

Some years ago on a train riding west, I read a whole newspaper page from the pen of Professor Lull of Yale, in which he declared that this body was nothing but a vestigial eye. He asserted that our mud-loving ancestors used to immerse their huge bodies in pools of slime and left this one eye above the same to look about for enemies, dangers, as well as friends and food. But in the process of time something evolved two eyes on opposite sides of the head, and so this little one, not being needful, went its way.

It is a small organ located in the roof of the third ventricle of the brain. Since Swale Vincent, professor of physiology of the University of London, says that "this gland is one of the most important organs in the entire body, and that it seems to control the inflow and outflow of the cerebro-spinal fluid of the third ventricle."

Is it any wonder that a leading Scientist, Dr. P. C. Mitchell, in Encyc. Britt., vol. 20, p. 33, recently said, "It is almost impossible to prove that any structure, however rudimentary, is useless, and, if it is in the slightest degree useful there is no reason why, on the hypothesis of direct creation, it should not have been created."

Sir Arthur Keith, in spite of his skepticism admits in the *British Medical Journal* of 1926,—"As our knowledge increases, the vestigial organs are decreasing."

Do you know, the profound pity expressed by immature students for those of us who are such backwoodsmen as to have reached identical conclusions with the most clever investigators, is small beside the deep sympathy we feel for that student who is taken advantage of in his third grade immaturity and is falsely instructed until he has secured his Ph.D., and sent out to be a propagandist of a philosophical lie that has to live by calling itself "scientific."

However, ignorance, or even educated infidelity, is not a preventative of justice, and for all such teachers

## JUDGMENT IS FORE-OR-DAINED

*This philosophy, like its predecessors, will perish.*

One hundred fifty years ago Deism was as popular in our schools as Darwinism is today. It had its marvellous exponents—Paine, Hume, Voltaire, Tyndall, Bolingbroke and Hobbs, but it now lies buried with their disintegrated bodies, and is not even so well known as are the names of its proponents, several of whom are familiar to the careful students of history only.

One thing certain, and, in consequence, cheering, is that a false philosophy must eventually fall. You can create an imitation of a man, and you can put inside of him a

23

machine and wind it up and make him walk; but he cannot walk far, and he will not walk long! His fall, when it occurs, will be a crash.

The greatest Scientists of Germany never accepted this philosophy.

Rudolph Virchow was in Germany what Saul was in Israel, head and shoulders above his fellow-scientists, and he never accepted the philosophy.

Bateson, who, until his recent death, was England's most outstanding man, gave an address in Toronto, that was a pratcical admission of all for which its opponents contend.

More, of Cincinnati, holds to scorn the idea that "the lowly Algæ evolved into a choir of angels."

A while ago, Austin Clark did not hesitate to confess the weaknesses of the philosophy.

The loud noise now being made in certain Universities by the smaller Scientists is only the rumble of machinery that is running down.

To be sure, professors have the immeasurable advantage of compulsory attendance upon what they have to say, and they take the additional advantage of creating, in the Universities, a rabid and egotistical atmosphere such as brow-beats the student who does not accept it, if not into acquiescence, at least into silence.

I have had it told me by students who do not accept the philosophy, that they feared to be its opponents lest they themselves be made the butt of further scorn and heckling.

The so-called Science that has to live after such a manner is certainly short-lived. You can coerce youth, but graduates become free men.

In my first debate on this subject against Professor Metcalf in the State College of North Carolina, I was backed up by four Alumni of the College, two of whom were attorneys, and all of whom had, in their maturity, flung away the tattered and decaying philosophy.

Speaking in Minneapolis before one of the Commercial Clubs one day, there were four graduates of the State University of Minnesota who told me, at the conclusion of the address, that it was their first time to listen to an argument against it, and that it was so conclusive that they were through with it forever.

In St. Louis two young women graduates of Eastern Universities, both of whom were ardent advocates of the philosophy, declined, when the Board invited me to speak in the Y.W.C.A., to make their appearance on the platform of the Y.W.C.A., of which they were Secretaries. They were converted by a single address, and in tears voiced their grief that they had even been led so far from God. The philosophy will perish.

*Its Prophets Will Finally Sleep Beneath the Sod.*

"*This year thou shalt die*" was said to Hananiah, the falst prophet. That is the sentence God has already passed upon a number of the present-day false prophets. They will perish this year.

Hume, Paine, and Voltaire, each prophesied the demise of Christianity; but they died without seeing it. They sleep in infidel graves, while the Cause of Christ sweeps on!

The conflict in the church is not at all a battle between Christians. It is a battle between the true believers in Christ and the followers of Chas. Darwin, some of whom cloak under the name Christian.

The Christian Century is one of the most radical of liberalistic journals, and yet, a few years ago, it frankly said this,

26

"Christianity according to Fundamentalism is one religion; Christianity according to Modernism is another religion; there is a clash here as profound and as grim as that between Christianity and Confusianism. Amiable words cannot hide the differences. The God of the Fundamentalist is one God; the God of the Modernist is another. The Christ of the Fundamentalist is one Christ; the Christ of the Modernist is another. The Bible of the Fundamentalist is one Bible; the Bible of the Modernist is another."

Certainly! Fortunately for Fundamentalists, our Christ has stood the test of 20 Centuries, and our Bible of thousands of years, while Modernism was born but yesterday, and is destined to breathe its last tomorrow. Time is God's agency for establishing the Truth, and it is equally His agency for bringing falsehood to its grave.

Christianity has an eternal advantage—*it gives to its converts the noblest ideas of living, and provides them with a bright expectation of life beyond.*

These basal facts are constitutional with Christianity, holding, as it does, that God created all, and is over all,

27

and that by His Spirit He is guiding in all. It expects of man, made in the Divine image, that he will, by divine help, reach divine ideals.

It is easy enough to make fun of Moses, and it is supposed to be very scholarly to deny his existence; but up to the present no Evolutionist has improved upon the decalogue. All those who repudiate these moral teachings bear in their bodies the mark of the Beast.

It is easy enough to talk of Jesus of Nazareth, and in seasoned and careful speech surreptitiously deny the Virgin Birth of the Christ, His Miracle working, His Atonement on Calvary's Cross, His Victory over the grave, His Ascension to the right hand of God, and His promised Second Coming! But, up to the present, Christ is the only Person who has proved an antidote to the moral leprosy of the world; the only Person who has so imparted His Spirit to the hearts of men as to affect clinics in regeneration; Christ is the only Person who has been able to convert the harlot into a saint, to sober the drunkard, and even change the murderer into a man of the tenderest mercies and the most considerate care of his fellows.

When the Science League of America was formed, Professor Ritter, president of Science Service, speaking in defense of Evolution, said,

"We must have a confidence in the natural that will not leave room for one jot or title of faith in the supernatural," so attempting to wipe out the Bible, to dispense with the claims of the Christ, and to ridicule from existence the hope of Heaven.

It is an ambitious program, I grant you; but it is a program that would blacken the world, reduce man to the level of the beast, and take even from the Christian himself that Blessed Hope of a personal fellowship with the saved, and an eternal residence in the Heaven which Christ declared He had gone to prepare for His own.

# W. B. RILEY'S FORTY VOLUMES

The Bible of the Expositor and the Evangelist

*Representing Thirty Years of Labor
Already Off the Press*

Cloth binding, per Vol....$1.00
Paper binding, per Vol.... .50

**Other Books by the Same Author**
*Larger Works*

Revival Sermons.........$1.50
My Bible, an Apologetic
　　　　　　　　　Cloth 1.00
Perennial Revival...Cloth 1.25
Seven New Testament Soul
　Winners .........Cloth 1.00
　　　　　　　　　Paper .50
The Blight of Unitarianism
　—a series of five sermons (postpaid)....... .25
God Hath Spoken........ 1.75
　(500 pages by the leading Bible expositors of the world. A text book on the Christian Fundamentals.)

# BOOKS BY DR. W. B. RILEY

Pastoral Problems...Cloth 1.00
The World's Only Hope
                   Cloth .75
Youth's Victory.....Cloth 1.00
                   Paper .60
Seven New Testament
  Soul-Winners ....Cloth 1.00
                   Paper .50
Wanted a World Leader
                   Paper .25
Philosophy of Father
  Coughlin ........Paper .25
The Victorious Life, Paper .25
Saved or Lost......Paper .25
Wives of the Bible..Cloth 1.00
Is Jesus Coming Again?
                   Cloth 1.00
Menace of Modernism
                   Paper .40
20—10 Cent Pamphlets... 1.00

### Order from
### IRENE WOODS
20 S. 11th St.
Minneapolis, Minn.

## 10c Booklets

The Doom of World Governments
Prophecy and the Red Russian Menace
Darwin's Philosophy and the Flood
Bloodless but Red
Are the Scriptures Scientific?
Evolution a False Philosophy
Theory of Evolution Tested by Mathematics
That Blessed Hope and the Resurrection Body
Humanism: Is It Also Heathenism?
The Church After 1900 Years
The Challenge of Youth
Christ and His City
Will Christ Come Again?
The Eclipse of Faith
The Interchurch, or the Kingdom by Violence
Redemption of the Downtown
Theological Liberty vs. License of Infidelity
Socialism in Our Schools
Is Society Rotting?
Civilization; Not Product of Evolution
All 20 Booklets to One Order, $1.00.

*Order from*
### L. W. CAMP
**1020 Harmon Place
Minneapolis, Minnesota**

# The Scientific Accuracy of the Sacred Scriptures

BY

### W. B. RILEY, D. D.
MINNEAPOLIS, MINN.

All rights reserved by
the Author

Price 10c per copy
" $ 7.50 per hundred
" $60.00 per thousand

# BOOKS BY DR. W. B. RILEY.

EVOLUTION OF THE KINGDOM, Revised Edition, paper 75c, cloth $1.50
THE PERENNIAL REVIVAL, cloth .............................. $1.00
THE CRISIS OF THE CHURCH, cloth .......................... 1.00
THE MENACE OF MODERNISM, paper 50c, cloth ............... 1.00
EPHESIANS, The Three-Fold Epistle, paper 40c, cloth ............ $0.75
Old Testament Types, paper ....................................... .40
The Gospel in Jonah, paper ....................................... .25
Daniel vs. Darwinism, paper ...................................... .25
Modern Amusements ............................................. .15
Jerusalem and the Jew ........................................... .10
The Challenge of Orthodoxy ..................................... .10
The Christian Confederacy ....................................... .10
Modernism in Baptist Schools .................................... .10
The Great Question, Who Was Christ? ........................... .10
The Eclipse of Faith ............................................. .10
Christian Science and Divine Healing ............................. .10
The Interchurch, or The Kingdom by Violence .................... .10
The Gospel for War Times ....................................... .10
Spiritualism, or Can We Commune With the Dead? ................ .15
Darwinism, or Is Man a Developed Monkey? ...................... .10
Speaking With Tongues .......................................... .05
Redemption of The Downtown .................................... .10

Order From
**DANA M. BERRY**

1006 Harmon Place,                                    Minneapolis, Minn.

# The Scientific Accuracy of the Sacred Scriptures
### By W. B. Riley, D. D.

"Thy word is true from the beginning" (Psa. 119:160), is an expression of the Psalmist that must be explained away before one can pit Science and the Sacred Scriptures against each other. Arthur Pierson thinks the Psalmist meant to say that from the first word, the Sacred Scriptures are true.

The modern method of study objects to any assumption. It insists that every theme and thing shall be subjected to whatever tests are essential in the establishment of its claims. To this, intelligent believers take no exception. If the Bible will not bear investigation; if scrutiny discloses shortcomings; if research disproves its assertions; if true Science discredits its clear claims, let it fall! We could forfeit it without a tear; join in digging its grave without regret, and return to the duties of life smitten by no serious bereavement.

True, it is serious business to discredit a book which has accomplished for the world what the Bible has wrought; but it would be more serious to believe a lie, or even to accept an irresponsible chart in making one's way over the sea of life. True, the Bible "was not written to show how the heavens go," but rather "how to go to heaven"; it is not a text book on "Science," but a guide book for "godly living." And yet, when it addresses itself at all to a subject of scientific concern, it should essentially speak the truth, if it makes the claim of inspiration! When we study the words of men, however wise they may be, we expect to come upon mistakes. When we read, and properly understand, what

"God hath spoken" we anticipate no such results. "Let God be found true; but every man a liar." "He that believeth not God hath made him a liar."

"But," we are told, "God has two books. One we call 'Nature,' the other 'Revelation'; He is just as certainly the author of the former as of the latter; one is the work of His hands and the other the fruit of His lips." What Jesus, when once he stooped down and wrote in the sand, expressed, we do not know. But can any man imagine that His writings in the sand were out of harmony with His spoken addresses? Is it possible that an all-wise God has produced in Nature and in Revelation contradictory volumes?

We have no fear whatever that the Scriptures must be maintained at the expense of Science; and we are fully persuaded that true Science will never be established at the cost of Scripture. The thing to be feared is, that the dust of false reasoning (of which the air is full today) will get into the eyes of men, and make it impossible for one to read from the Sacred Page, and for another to see the meaning of the open book of Nature; and so, for either, to discern the perfect agreement between God's Word and God's Work.

First of all, then, let us give

## THE DEFINITION OF THE TERMS INVOLVED.

**What is Science?** Can we improve upon the Standard Dictionary's statement—"Knowledge gained and verified by exact observation and correct thinking; especially as methodically formulated and arranged in a rational system"? That definition takes you at once out of the realm of speculation. It disposes of such terms as "theory" and "hypothesis," making them possible servants of Science, but never its synonyms. It is admitted that almost every assertion made in the name of Science a hundred years since, is now out of date; and, while this clearly demonstrates our progress, it also suggests that we are still in the hypothetical and theoretical stage. No one would dispute that Sir Isaac Newton was somewhat of a scientist; nor yet that Tyndall was equally worthy the name; and yet when they take exactly opposite positions concerning the refraction of light, both may be wrong, but both cannot be right. Huxley and Darwin are names that somehow sit easily together in the same sentence, and yet these men, working in almost the same realm, are not always in agreement. The explanation is easy—"the verification of knowledge by exact observation and correct thinking" is the highest accomplishment of which the human mind is capable, and not every man who cries "Eureka" has found it. This is not to inveigh against the sincerity of investigators, nor even to deride their conclusions, but only to call attention to the most patent fact of their experience! "Knowledge, gained and verified by exact observation and correct thinking," will never be overthrown by mortal men, nor yet by God. God would dethrone Himself by such an endeavor! True Science will stand!

**What is Scripture?** Paul defines "all Scripture" as that which is "God-breathed," and the process of it is "that holy men of old spake as they were moved (or borne along) by the Holy Ghost"! Knowing himself to be of that company, Paul affirms, "We speak not in words which man's wisdom teacheth, but which the Spirit teacheth; combining spiritual things with spiritual words." If one runs through the Old Testament he will find God everywhere assuming the Authorship of the Sacred Scriptures. The phrases are like these, "The Lord spake unto Moses saying," "These are the words of the covenant which the Lord commanded Moses to make with the children of Irael"; "The Lord spake unto Joshua"; "The words of the commandment of the Lord," etc. Not scores, but hundreds of times, does God claim to be the Author of both the thought and the language of the Holy Book. David declares, "The Spirit of the Lord spake by me, and His word was in my tongue." (2 Sam. 23:2.) To me it is the most remarkable evidence of the skepticism of the age that because there are some difficulties in the theory of Verbal Inspiration, men are willing to throw it away, and adopt such notions as are now current, to the effect that God simply stimulated the thought, but did not determine the speech; that some parts of the Bible are literally true, and others are only allegory; that some are fact, others only fiction; that some are to be treated with credence and others with criticism; that all must come to the test of one's "inner consciousness," and, at that court, be either accepted or rejected.

The same men who so define "Inspiration" or "illumination," or whatever it is, would go into court tomorrow to insist upon the settlement of an estate, in which they were named as heirs, on a **verbal basis.** They would call the attention of attorneys and judge to what was "written," and unless they had some unrighteous end to be conserved, they would permit no departure from **the very words** in which the testator expressed himself. It is little wonder, therefore, that the New Testament writers, who may be conceded to have known what the Scriptures were, refer to the Old Testament more than eighty times, as that "which is written." Never once did they abandon the verbal interpretation of the same.

6

If the words of the Old Testament were "the words of God," perhaps no believer, at least, will dispute that the New Testament stands upon the same level. And so the Bible does not "contain the Scriptures,"—the Bible is the Scriptures —God's revealed Word, which can hardly have been given to men with less care than any intelligent, faithful father would show in framing the article that bequeathed his possessions to his children. If, in civil courts, the lightest word of the testator is the weightiest law, who will dare to treat with contempt, thought or phrase found in the Divine Will?

Mark you, there is a decided difference between the plain statement of the Sacred Scriptures and some absurd opinion. It may be, that in the centuries of the past an uninstructed Christian conceived the world as having a flat surface, the sky as a roof, and the stars as holes through the same. Kepler, who was something of a scientist, once expressed the conviction that the world was a living animal. Is that assertion to be confounded with Science? Fanciful interpretations in the one realm are just as common as in the other; and they neither prove nor disprove anything. I do not have to harmonize the Scriptures with the absurd statements of every man who may speak in the name of Science; and I do not have to harmonize Science with the assertions of every man who may mistakenly appeal to Moses, or even to Christ. Science is God's voice in Nature; the Scriptures are God's voice in grace, and it does not fall to the lot of any mortal man to harmonize them; the harmony is in Him. He cannot contradict Himself!

To say the least, it is a strange procedure when a man proclaims as his theme, "The Harmony between Science and Scripture," and then shows how that comes to pass by just quietly disposing of the latter; by saying, for instance, that the first chapter of Genesis is "the best that Moses knew,—the impression of that early age, but a mistake none the less." Is that harmony? Is it not, rather, annihilation? It may let you out of your difficulty, but you escape at the expense of inspiration; and to the unspeakable loss of the people. There used to be an eccentric preacher in Kentucky well known to the author. He did no great amount of study, and yet he commonly preached with unction. One day he found himself before an audience with no unction on hand; even thoughts refused to come. He floundered through a few ill-formed sentences, and then, squarely facing his audience, he said, "Brethren and sisters, you think I have got into the brush and can't get out, don't you? Well, I'll show you; we'll just look to the Lord and be dismissed"! But let it be understood that when you dismiss the claims of the Sacred Book and walk out of your difficulties, you have lost the divine message and left the hungry multitudes unsatisfied.

**GENESIS IN SCIENCE AND SCRIPTURE.**

It will scarcely be disputed that so far as men have seen any inharmony between the Sacred Scriptures and Science, the first chapter of Genesis has been made the storm center. On that account I invite your attention to this part of the Word, and dare the assertion that its careful study, instead of demonstrating the inharmony between Science and Scripture, will reveal the most undreamed of agreement in these great books of God.

First of all, **think of the argument from fifteen facts in order.**

First fact, in order—God created the heavens; second fact—"and the earth"; third—water; fourth—light; fifth—firmament; sixth—grass; seventh—herb; eighth—tree; ninth—appearance of heavenly bodies; tenth—fish; eleventh—moving things; twelfth—fowls; thirteenth—creeping things; fourteenth—cattle; fifteenth—man!

Now, the latest science will consent to this order of creation. The heavens were certainly made first; the earth certainly made second; water certainly appeared third; light, fourth; firmament next; grass thereafter; the manifestation of sun and moon, ninth; the appearance of fish—tenth; moving things—eleventh; fowls—twelfth; creeping things—thirteenth; cattle, etc., fourteenth, and last—man.

Other writers have called attention to the unspeakable significance of this order when considered before the laws of permutation. The Standard Dictionary says, "The number of permutations of any given number of things, taken all at a time, is equal to the product of the natural numbers from one up to the number given, inclusive."

Now, if Moses only spake the science of his times, he knew practically nothing of the order of creation. Consequently he must guess at it. He must guess whether the heavens or the earth were first formed. In his day no man imagined that the heavenly bodies were bigger than the earth and all men supposed that they moved about it. How then does it happen that Moses, when he came to guess which was first formed, the heavens or the earth, mentioned the heavens in the primary place? You say, "Well, it was an easy accident, since there was only one other alternative." Did you ever hear the story of the Irishman who, meeting a neighbor, said, "We have a fine baby at our house this marnin'." "What is it?" asked the interested friend. "Guiss"!

9

"A girl," said the neighbor. "No, sir; guiss agin"! "A boy." "Now, who's bin tellin' ye?" To be sure, Moses had but one chance out of two on this arrangement. But he got it right!

Third fact—the appearance of water. Here Moses' task was not so easy, for it was not one in three, but one in six, according to the law of permutation. It could have been the heavens, first; water, second; earth, third—but that was not true. It could have been the earth first, water second and the heavens third—but that was not true. It could have been water first, the earth second, the heavens last, but that was not true. It could have been the earth first and the heavens second and the water last, but that was not true. In other words, there are six different arrangements of these relations, 1-2-3, 1-3-2, 2-1-3, 2-3-1, 3-2-1, 3-1-2. But Moses somehow struck the right one. A good guesser! Introduce light and you make twenty-four such relations. Moses hit it again. One chance in twenty-four, but he was the lucky man.

When you get to the fifth, you have 120 possible orders. Strange to say, Moses does not miss it!

When you get to the sixth, you have 720. In other words there are 719 chances against you. But Moses got it right!

When you get to the seventh, you have 5,040. In other words, 5,039 chances against him. But Moses hit it!

When you get to the eighth you have 40,320. Not a glorious prospect of striking it straight, but still Moses accomplishes it!

When you get to the ninth you only have one chance in 362,880!

When you get to the tenth you have only one chance in 3,628,800!

10

When you get to the eleventh, 39,916,800. When you get to the fifteenth, one chance in 1,307,674,367,900. And yet, strange to say, in the whole arrangement, he never misses!

Go dig up Bob Ingersoll, and give the poor fellow a chance to apologize for ever having spoken of the "mistakes of Moses." Bob should not come alone.

But this is not the end. We make bold to assert that from the beginning to the end of Genesis, 1st Chapter, there is not a blunder from a scientific standpoint. It is scientific that the heavens were created first, and the earth second. The very latest science would tell you that the earth was "waste and void" and the "darkness" resulting from the nebulous state, "was upon the face of the deep." For a long time Science spoke of the third verse of Genesis as certainly involving a mistake, "And God said, Let there be light and there was light." This, in advance of the appearance of the sun, supposed to be the only source of light; but finally La Place declared it to be a scientific certainty, that in the condensation of the originally formless chaos, there was such molecular and chemical action as must have emitted great volumes of light. No wonder Boardman, in his "Creative Week," says, "Why will the Academy vote Moses a blunderer for declaring that light existed before the sun appeared, and yet vote La Place a scientist for affirming precisely the same thing"?

The next point of scientific attack was upon the fifth verse, "And there was evening, and there was morning, one day." It was boldly asserted that Moses supposed all this change from chaos to cosmos took place in twenty-four hours. But mark you, Moses does not refer to twenty-four hours at all! "From evening to morning" is only twelve hours. You will not have finished this chapter before it is made perfectly clear that Moses is not speaking of twenty-four hour days. He knew the law of herbs, yielding seed after their kind, and trees bearing fruit after their kind; and these things are not accomplished in a day. It took seasons to produce fruit, and even many years, to mature trees and make them reproductive. And yet that whole process he mentions as in the third day. Again Moses names three successive days before the sun and moon appear. Without the sun's rays to mark off a twenty-four hour day, a solar day is impossible. What is God's Day, according to the Bible? In the second chapter, the entire creation, from start to finish, is mentioned as having occurred in a day. It could not, therefore, according to Moses, mean twenty-four hours. **What is a "yom" with God?** Peter tells us "One day is with the Lord as a thousand years." (2 Pet. 3:8) Moses, himself, in the nineteenth Psalm, declares that "a thousand years in God's sight were but as yesterday when it is passed, and as a watch in the night," and that he is speaking of this very period is evident in the context, where he says, "Before the mountains were brought forth and Thou gavest birth to the earth and the world, even from everlasting to everlasting (from Olam to Olam: or, era to era) Thou art God."

But surely Moses was mistaken in the eighth verse, "And God called the firmament heaven"? Even Mr. Huxley slipped here, by charging Moses with believing that the heaven was a solid substance, resting like a canopy over the earth. But Mr. Huxley was not a Hebrew scholar; hence his mistake. The Hebrew word translated "firmament" means "expanse." Can you improve it by your latest scientific expression?

The ninth verse also reveals the remarkable wisdom vouchsafed to this man, "Let the waters under the heaven be gathered together in one place, and let the dry land appear." There was not a man in the earth at that time that knew, or could have known, that all the seas were linked together, whereas the continents are divided. But exploration has proven it. Dana, in his Manual of Geology, says that while the continents are separated, the seas occupy one bed. As to the order of the appearance of life, Genesis and geology are exactly together, beginning with grass, and ending with man. There is not a geological mistake in Genesis.

Equally remarkable is the fact that instead of speaking of the sun and moon as giving their light from the first, Moses holds back their rays until the fourth day; at which time he does not declare they were created, for that belonged in the opening sentence, "In the beginning God created the heavens" —but they were made to "divide the day from the night," "and to be for signs and for seasons and for days and for years." Many scientists believe that the earth took on its present angle of axis at this very period in its development, when it cooled to the point where the vapors condensed and fell upon it as water. And we know that without that axis-angle, determining its relation to the sun and moon, our seasons would fail, and we would return to an ice-age!

Now, as to whether the law of generation as set forth in Genesis, "every seed after its kind," is true, or whether the origin of species is by "natural selection," the whole weight of discovery is with Genesis and against Darwin. The truth of Genesis, we know, from the lowest form of grass to soulful man; everything is bringing forth "after its kind." We have seen that law executed tens of thousands of times and in millions of forms. The creation of a new species, by natural selection, no man has ever yet seen. Why, therefore, should we imagine that there is any conflict between Scripture and Science? At every point where it is possible to institute a comparison that is reliable, an utter agreement appears. The rocks, from the lowest stratum to the last laid down, confirm the facts of God's creative week.

"A glory gilds the Sacred page,
Majestic like the sun,
It gives a light to every age,
It gives but borrows none.

The hand that gave it still supplies
The gracious light and heat;
His truths upon the nations rise,
They rise, but never set."

Permit me to mention some other **inexplicable instances of Science in Scripture.** Harvey, in modern times, discovered the circulation of the blood, and declared its relation to life. Moses affirmed it three thousand years ago, "The life is in the blood." You have heard Galileo glorified for having discovered that this part of the universe was heliocentric and not geocentric, as the ancients supposed; and Newton honorably mentioned for his great discovery of the law of gravitation. The Scriptures declared both a few thousand years before these brethren were born. Job declared of the dayspring, that it "takes hold of the ends of the earth; it is turned as clay to the seal" (38:13), and as for gravitation, while scientists and churchmen alike were adopting theories of the earth's support, akin to the old maps and atlases some of us used to carry to school showing Atlas holding up the world by his huge shoulders, or akin to that which the Hindus

14

now hold, namely, that it was a flat plane, with possible stories above and below, held up by the heads of elephants, with their tails turned out, and their feet resting on the shell of an immense tortoise, and the tortoise in turn on the coil of a snake, Job was remonstrating in these words, "He hangeth the earth upon nothing" (26:7)—the very deliverance of your latest Science!

It is only in very modern times that any man imagined the atmosphere to have any weight, and we still employ the phrase, "light as air," and yet we know that it has a weight of fifteen pounds to every square inch; and modern science could almost tell you exactly what was the awful pressure upon the face of the globe twenty-five thousand miles in circumference. This, however, was not information to the Old Testament writers! Job, one of the most ancient of them all, says of God, that "He makes a weight for the wind; yea, he meteth out the waters by measure." Galileo discovered that air has gravity; but thirty centuries before him, Job affirmed the same. It would seem, therefore, that inspiration is as accurate as experimentation.

It is only within a few years that weather bureaus have had any occasion; that men imagined storms of cloud and wind, and waves of heat and cold obeyed unchangeable laws, and might, therefore, be tabulated and reported even in advance of their arrival. But Solomon understood it and wrote long since, in Ecclesiastes 1:6. "The wind goeth toward the south and turneth about unto the north. It turneth about continually in its course, and the wind returneth again to its circuits." It is only by modern discovery that men imagined that there were other sounds than those which our ears catch; but now we know that when we pass thirty-eight thousand vibrations per second, the ear cannot follow, and every heavenly body, in its motions, is making music, so that Job was not mistaken when he declared "the morning stars sang together," nor David when he declared of Jehovah, "Thou makest the morning and the evening to rejoice."

Arthur Pierson, after having called attention to some of these remarkable instances of agreement, says Shakespeare was right when he wrote:

"There's not the smallest orb which thou beholdest,
But in his motion, like an angel sings,
Still choiring to the young eyed cherubim.
Such harmony is in immortal souls;
But whilst this muddy vesture of decay
Doth grossly close it in, we cannot hear it."

But the most remarkable instance of Scripture anticipation of science was the late discovery of T. N. A., the highest explosive ever known or conceived.

It was conceded from the beginning of the late world war, that the alliance discovering the highest explosive would win. Two young Americans—chemists—set themselves to that task. Knowing that snow and hail were contractions formed at 32 degrees above zero, while ice formed at thirty above and became an expansion, they took the explosive chemicals in liquid state and crystallized them by the temperature of hail and snow and lo, the result was a terror and Germany surrendered. Then for the first time men knew what Job meant when he wrote 3500 years ago, saying, "Hast thou entered into the treasures of the snow, or hast thou seen the treasures of the hail, which I have reserved against the time of trouble, against the day of battle and war?" Job 38:22.

We candidly believe that if the men who are spending much time in seeing what can be said against the Scriptures, should assume a friendly attitude and search with a kindred diligence for its remarkable defenses, they could find them with utter ease, and would be shortly confirmed in the "faith once delivered" and able to boast with the poet:

> "I paused one day beside the blacksmith's door
> And listened to the anvil ring the evening's chime.
> And looking in, I saw upon the floor
> Old hammers, worn with beating years of time.
>
> 'How many anvils have you had,' said I,
> 'To wear and batter out these hammers so?'
> 'Just one,' he answered, with a twinkling eye,
> 'The anvil wears the hammers out, you know.'
>
> And so, I thought, the Anvil of God's Word
> For ages skeptic blows have beat upon;
> Yet, though the noise of infidel was heard,
> The anvil is unworn—the hammers, gone!"

## SOME POINTS WHERE COMPARISON IS IMPOSSIBLE.

Not to all subjects to which Science speaks do the Scriptures address themselves. It is equally true that the Scriptures discuss many subjects with which Science has naught to do. There are points in human experience where the microscope, the scalpel, the telescope tell us nothing. They transcend all scientific investigation! And yet that problem is not more difficult than are the problems of sin, substitution and salvation.

A man may easily say that Moses was mistaken when he declared how sin came into the world. But who will attempt to demonstrate it, and how? We know that sin is here. The Bible affirms that it came through an evil spirit; that man accepted his suggestion and continues to accept it, and so suffers the penalty of violated law. Who has presented a saner explanation of sin?

It is the height of folly to speak of "the Scriptures as teaching that the innocent must suffer for the sins of the guilty," "that children are condemned because of their parents' blunder." It never hints such a thing, and it never did! The second commandment does not say that God is visiting the iniquities of the fathers upon their innocent children, but it does affirm that "judgment falls upon the third and fourth generation of them that hate him," and why shouldn't it, unto generations of generations? Shall men hate God and escape judgment? The law, when first declared, was, "The soul that sinneth, it shall die." Is not that law righteous? The Scriptures are very careful to follow that statement with another from the pen of Ezekiel, "The son shall not bear the iniquity of the father; neither shall the father bear the iniquity of the son. The righteousness of the righteous shall be upon him; and the wickedness of the wicked shall be upon him." (Ezek. 19:20.)

It may be easy enough to set up untenable theories of sin, and assign them either to the Sacred Scriptures, or to the conservative defenders of the same, when neither have ever spoken aught to warrant such caricature. I have been in the ministry over thirty years. My daily associations, of an intrinsic character, have been with the conservative wing of the church, and in that entire time I have never heard Jehovah described as a God who visited the sins of guilty parents upon the heads of innocent children, by any one of them. On the contrary, they have depicted Jehovah as a God of infinite love, punishing no innocent men or women; even pitying the sinner and proffering him grace in Jesus Christ. Will the man who sets himself up as a student of Science, and a preacher of the Sacred Scriptures, object; and if so, has he a better view of God to present?

Again, if the God who breathed upon the waste of a darkened world, and converted its chaos into cosmos, and quickened its death into life, is willing to do the same for a man "dead in trespasses and sins," will men object? Cannot He of whom Milton sang

"Thou from the first
Wast present, and with mighty wings outstretched,
Dove-like, sat'st brooding on the vast abyss,
And madest it pregnant,"

quicken our dead souls that they shall live again? If we cannot bind the influence of the Pleiades, shall we attempt to set limits to the work of God's own Spirit, or demand that He bring His endeavors within the limits of natural explanation?

Is it not written, "Except one be born of water and the Spirit, he cannot enter into the Kingdom of God. And that which is born of the flesh is flesh; and that which is born of the Spirit is spirit," and are we not enjoined to "marvel not" about it, since "the wind bloweth where it will, and thou hearest the voice thereof, but knowest not whence it cometh and whither it goeth," and told, "so is every one that is born of the Spirit?"

Just how it happens that the drunken man who staggers into a sanctuary and listens to the Gospel of the Son of God, and goes out, never to drink again, supported, in his new sobriety, by the sense of Divine Love, Science may never be able to explain; but that does not disprove what you and I have seen in the clinic of regeneration.

Just how it happens that the woman who has walked in the ways of wickedness, is suddenly roused to repentance by the rehearsal of the Divine goodness, scientists may not even see, but the Son of Man rejoices and the angels are made happy by the sight of His face. You can deny the direct creation of man in the divine image, if you like, but you will never be able to disprove it. You may deny the unity of the race, but even there the evidences are against you; you may deny the description of the fall, but sin remains unexplained. You may deny that there is any supernaturalism, and yet, as against that, we say that he who starts along the path clearly marked in Sacred Scripture will go from sin to salvation; from salvation to sanctification and from sanctification to the eternal fellowship of the Father.

Years ago we went through the Hoosac Tunnel for the first time. Did you ever hear how it was constructed? There started two companies of men to work on opposite sides of the mountain, but the survey had been so accurately made that when the men met midway, the approaching walls of the excavations were not an inch off the line. But the man who wants to turn home to God and heaven has more than an accurate line marked by survey; he has a well beaten road lying full before him. Others have gone over it by the thousands; yea, by the millions, and as the prodigal who trudged his way back to the farm house from which he had been so long separated, by a well-traveled road, found his father coming forth to meet him, so shall the lost man find God if he but turn his feet to the path upon which there falls the light of this Book—the Bible!

# The Theory of Evolution Tested by Mathematics

*By* W. B. Riley

# W. B. RILEY'S FORTY VOLUMES

The Bible of the Expositor and the Evangelist

*Representing Thirty Years of Labor*

THIRTY-THREE VOLUMES
ALREADY OFF THE PRESS

Cloth binding (Mailing 15 cents extra) .................................$1.00
Paper binding (Mailing 10 cents extra) ....................................... .50

**Other Books by the Same Author**

*Larger Works*

Revival Sermons ........................$1.50
Ten Burning Questions (new), cloth ....................................... 1.50
Inspiration or Evolution, paper 75c; 2nd edition............Cloth 1.25
Crisis of the Church, cloth......... 1.25
The Blight of Unitarianism (New) a series of five sermons, (postpaid) ..................... .50
God Hath Spoken ...................... 1.75
 (500 pages by the leading Bible expositors of the world. A text book on the Christian Fundamentals.)

*(Continued outside back cover)*

# The Theory of Evolution Tested by Mathematics

*"No lie is of the truth."* 1 John 2:21

### By W. B. Riley

This text constitutes a truism. "No lie is of the truth," is the most self-evident of all statements, and on that account it becomes a touchstone for theories, proven and unproven alike. If they are of the truth they are not a lie; and if they are lies they are not of the truth. There is one point at least at which all investigators ought to be agreed and that is in the love of truth. Here, surely, Christianity and Science can come together. The Scientist always professes to be in search of truth; Christianity demands the truth of its advocates, and reminds them that truth is the way to freedom; that truth is the Saviour; that truth is a chief characteristic of God himself. There is not an intelligent Christian in the world who does not stand ready to accept the truth at any cost, and at all cost. Galileo was a believer. That is why he was willing to suffer for the truth. Sir Isaac

Newton was a believer. That is why he endured unpopularity for truth's sake. Kepler was a believer and an effective minister. That is why, in all his discoveries, he conceived himself as thinking God's thoughts after Him.

The theory of evolution was born of Grecian philosophy, but, in the sifting to which time subjects speculations, it was dropped, and for nearly three thousand years left on the ash heap of forgotten vagaries. Its temporary revival by Erasmus Darwin was a comparative failure; but his grandson Charles succeeded in recovering it to attention, and since 1859 that attention has constantly increased.

However, its advocates who assert that it is "now a demonstrated science" are animated by the same spirit that leads the small boy to whistle as he passes through the dark woods, namely an attempt to keep courage up.

In previous deliverances on this subject we have shown that the theory was not a science, as it was utterly without verification. We have also shown that even its advocates disagree upon practically every step supposed to have been taken by nature's processes. But at this time we propose to go on the aggressive and demonstrate by

4

Mathematics—the exact science—the utter falsity of the whole philosophy.

It will be conceded, we think, that the mathematical test is an acid one, and if the theory falls before it, its obsequies should immediately follow.

I am going to arrange what I have to say in this lecture around The Theory Tested, The Realm of Anthropology, and The Truth Triumphant.

## The Theory Tested

*Already we have recorded the confession of failure at the point of evidence.*

It will not be necessary for me to go over that ground again. When men are asked to believe that dead matter gave birth to even so low a form of life as an amoeba, and that eventuated in some marine animal form, which in turn evolved into amphibian, later to a reptile and then into birds and animals, some of which, in turn, became monkeys and finally either the monkey, or his ancestor, arrived at manhood, and no proofs are forthcoming for any single point in the process and no missing links can be presented in demonstration of the same, he is either an infant in intellect, or so sadly immature as to be irresponsible, if he accept such unproven and unprovable conclusions.

5

Sir William Dawson, the great Canadian geologist, said

"No case is certainly known in human experience, where any species of animal or plant has been so changed as to assume all the characteristics of a new species."

Prof. Vernon Kellogg, of Leland Stanford University, in his " Darwinism of Today " says,

"Speaking by and large, we only tell the general truth when we declare that no indubitable cases of species forming, or transforming, that is, of descent, have been observed. For my part it seems better to go back to the old and safe ignoramus standpoint."

Prof. H. H. Neuman, of Chicago University, a man whose statements in defense of evolution border on the daffy, when asked by Dr. Williams, "How many new species have arisen in the last 6000 years?" wrote this evasive reply: "I do not know how to answer your question. None of us know just what a species is!"

When Dr. Osborn, of Columbia University, N. Y., was questioned after the same manner, R. C. Murphy, his assistant, answered, "From every point of view, your short note of August 22nd raises questions which no scientific man can possibly answer. We have very little knowledge as to just when any particular species of animal arose," while Dr. J. B. Warren, of the University of California, said

"If the theory of evolution be true, then, during many thousands of years, covered in whole or in part by present human knowledge, there would certainly be known at least a few instances of the evolution of one species from another. No such instance is known."

*The evolutionist's rendezvous of illimitable time is destroyed by the mathematical test.*

The dear boys and girls of high schools and Universites have listened to the parading of "eons" with which the Darwinites have filled their quivers, until they think no longer in terms of time, but only in that of eternity.

For instance, when Prof. Osborn says, "If man was known on the earth thirty millions of years ago he was then much like he is now," the children do not revolt.

When Prof. Neuman wants us to believe that it is at least sixty millions of years since life appeared on earth, the uninstructed may be a bit astounded, but they fear to protest the Professor's infallible (?) information.

All such ages on ages of time are not

7

only poor speculation, but travesties of thought when considered in the light of facts. It is not at all likely that animal life appeared on the earth a few millions of years before the sun had an existence, and the age of the sun is in decided dispute as between scientists. For instance, James Jeans, in "The Stars in their Course," speaks of "two hundred million years" having intervened since the sun threw off its satellites. But the Helmholtz contraction theory would make the sun only some twenty million years of age, and the earth, of course, much younger.

Lord Kelvin, easily one of the greatest of modern scientists, regarded the sun not over eighteen to twenty million years of age, while all those arguments that have been put up for the extreme age of the earth are perishing one by one.

Lord Kelvin taught that the earth's crust did not call for more than 8,302,000 years; and Kelvin reached his conclusion by scientific processes; he did not rest the same in mere guess.

Charles Lyell, geologist in Darwin's day, declared that the delta of the Mississippi was 100,000 years in its formation; while the Coast Scientific Survey fixed it at 4,400.

But while there is no present possibility for knowing either the age of the sun or the earth, there is a perfect argument against evolution in what we do know.

If we concede that life, on the earth, originated 60,000,000 years ago, perhaps 40,000,000 years before the sun itself existed, and 52,000,000 to 53,000,000 years before the earth was formed, still the theory breaks down by the law of mathematics. 3,000,000 of species, developing in 60,000,000 years, by the law of mathematics, would give us over 2000 of them in the last 6000 years.

Dr. William Williams, in his little volume on this subject, says: "Twenty doublings of the first species of animals that originated, give us 1,048,576 species, therefore an average of each of the twenty doublings would take 1/20 of the 60,000,000 years, or 3,000,000 years for its development, and one half of the entire 1,048,576 or 524,288 species to have originated within the last 3,000,000 years; and since the number of species must have increased in geometrical ratio, 2097 species must have originated within the last 6000 years, an average of one new species of animal every three years."

Now, how do the facts fare before this acid test of mathematics? It has been admitted not only by the followers of Charles Darwin, but by Darwin himself, that not one new species has risen in that time. Mr. Darwin says,

"In spite of all the efforts of trained observers, not one change of one species into another is on record."

Where the 2097 should be known, as recorded by the observations of man, not a single instance appears! How absurd to maintain Darwin's philosophy in the face of that mathematical fact. The rendezvous of time, even though we stretch life on the earth to 60,000,000 of years or 40,000,000 to 42,000,000 of years beyond the formation of the sun, we still fail to find, in this infinity of imagination, one solitary proof for the Darwin philosophy.

A very natural question is this, "Why, in view of these things do the professors in the schools continue to teach it?"

The answer is not simple, it is rather complex! There are many and varied factors that enter into this infatuation.

First and foremost among these, according to the Questionnaire put out by Prof. Lueba, over one half the professors along these lines are atheists. They cannot afford to consent to the creation theory, for that would compel recognition of God.

The second factor that comes into this farcical performance is the circumstance that many of the minority who still retain some sort of a god, fear to oppose their unbelieving brethren, who in most institutions, hold the higher station and are supposed to be the leaders in scientific investigation.

Still further, a great many of these professors are the authors of one or more text books, committed to the evolution hypothesis, and that text book does not sell on its merits but by State enforcement, at double the cost of production and is a magnificent addition to the comparatively small salary paid the professor in this special department where this theory is involved.

And still further, when a man has once committed himself to a theory in a book, and that book is having a fair, even though it is an enforced sale, he cannot repudiate the theory and save his face.

The newspapers told us a few days since that the chief difficulty in the Japo-Chinese trouble was to save the face of the contestants. That is the chief difficulty in the controversy that has raged about evolution. There are thousands of scientists, who if they prayed at all, would devoutly pray to die rather than be compelled to surrender to the prophets of Christianity, and admit that this castle in the air stands upon imaginary foundation. They have put so much into it, and lifted its cupolas to such imaginary heights, that they dread the day when

11

the whole thing crashes and carries down their reputations for truth and ends their profit from text books sold at twice and three times the cost of printing; and above all, shames them in the presence of the misguided students who, in their infancy and immaturity, have followed to the very day of disaster and chagrin.

But to show you still further the untenableness of this philosophy let us enter for a while

### THE REALM OF ANTHROPOLOGY

Here the Science of Mathematics bears the most eloquent testimony to the truthfulness of Scripture, and renders the most damaging testimony against the Evolutionary Hypothesis.

To illustrate: *First it speaks of the location of original man.*

The Bible, by the pen of Moses, places that location in the Garden of Eden, in Mesopotamia, on the Tigris and Euphrates Rivers.

Dr. Wm. A. Williams says, "Suppose the Garden of Eden to be 100 miles wide and 125 miles long, or 12,500 square miles. There are 4,005 such areas in the habitable globe (computing only those central attractive portions). If Moses were a mere guesser, he would have 4,004 opportunities to miss it."

Here again Science has been compelled to certify to the truthfulness of Scripture. There are more high class Scientists who believe that man originated in Mesopotamia than hold to any other single theory. To be sure, some have said, "Not so, he started in Europe." Others, "His beginnings were in Africa," and for a time, at least, the pig tooth discovered by Harold Cook in Nebraska, and mistaken by leading Scientists for a human tooth, led some to insist that man originated on the American Continent. All evidences to date, however, are in favor of Mesopotamia.

When we begin to study human language, it works its way slowly, but certainly, back to that center.

The Sumerian language is among the most ancient, and its discovered fragments are in that region. In fact, every great discovery in ancient and buried languages pushes us toward that center, and gives good occasion to Prof. Max Müller's contention that "all languages are derived from one."

*Religion also bears a confirming testimony.* As we push it back to the dawn of well-known history we find it set in the Mesopotamian vicinity, and although the original revelation, made of God to Adam and Eve, was shortly corrupted, the solitary feature recorded in Genesis as the Divine demand characterizes even the corrupt forms, namely, the sacrifice of animals with the idea that the shed blood atoned for sin. That feature is in every ancient oriental religion.

It is a confirmation of both the revelation given to man and the symbolic significance of such blood, as a type of the Lamb, destined to be finally slain on Calvary's Cross.

At present there are hundreds of forms of religion. They reach every degree of degradation, but the further back you push them the smaller their number becomes, and the more unified is the Faith of man.

Both these facts, when applied to anthropology, combine to double the arithmetic certainty of Scripture statement, and to dispute the claims of Evolution which require man to originate in many portions of the world at practically the same time, to start out with a multiplicity of tongues, and from the first to have a variety of religions as large in number as was the development of monkeys into men.

Again, Mendel's law rests upon the mathematical precision that according to it, if man was an evolution of the lower animal life, the alleged recessive brute ancestor would be constantly coming forward to claim certain of his off-spring, and young apes, or whatever forms our brute ancestors took, would be born to women; but in the 6000 to 7000 years of well-known human history, no such an exhibit of the Mendelian law has occurred.

Little wonder that Prof. J. Arthur Thompson of A b e r d e e n, Evolutionist though he is, should feel led to write:

"Modern research is leading us away from the picture of primitive man as brutish, dull, lascivious and bellicose. There is more justification for regarding primitive man as clever, kindly, adventurous and inventive."

Little wonder that Prof. A. H. Sayce of Oxford University should say:

"As far back as the monuments carry us, we find a highly-developed art, a highly organized government, and a highly-educated people."

*The Origin of Languages Bears Testimony for Mathematical Precision.*

The number of languages in the world are not great enough to require more history than sweeps in between us and Noah. The American Indian is not supposed to have been on this Continent, at least in direct relation to the existing Indian tribes,

15

longer than 4,000, or at the most, 4,500 years; and yet in that time this one people had developed about 200 languages and dialects. Multiply this by the several Continents, separated as they are by wide seas, and you account for every language and dialect in existence within the easy limit of 4,500 years, or the time since the Flood.

The same principle may be applied to the peoples themselves. The racial differences are not so great as to require a million years for their developments. On the other hand they could all have easily risen from the three sons of Noah,—Shem, Ham, and Japheth. I had six children, born to a blonde mother and a brunette father. Their variety in size and color could easily account for six nations if separated on separate continents for five thousand years. Dr. Davenport, famed in America as an Evolutionist, says that no people of English descent are more absently related than 30th cousin, and yet, there is a great variety in the English family, produced according to Prof. Conklin by not more than 32 generations.

How strange Prof. Conklin's view then, that men might have originated on the earth more than two million years ago, or 60,000 generations away. Such a view finds no defense in either our racial differences, our language differentiations or our varieties of religion.

But, I come to the most important point in this argument, namely—

*The Arithmetical Test of the Earth's Population.*

Here again I want to acknowledge my indebtedness to the little book from the pen of Dr. Wm. A. Williams. The Bible shows that about 5,077 years ago two people married. Noah took unto himself a wife, and when Noah was 500 years of age he had three sons—Shem, Ham, and Japheth. The revelation was made to him that the world, if it continued in its iniquity and impenitence, was to be drowned with a flood; and in the 7th and 8th chapters of Genesis we have a full record of that catastrophe.

That record is not only a matter of plainly written history, but is confirmed by traditions found with every nation on the earth.

These facts alone would seem to leave little question of its historicity and utter accuracy; but fortunately the acid test of mathematics can be best applied at this point.

If the race started over with two people 5,077 years ago, we can tell within a few thousand how many people ought to be found on the face of the earth at any given time. Our basis of measurement in this matter is the Jewish nation. We know when and how it originated, and can reckon from the day of Jacob's marriage until the present moment.

According to Hales, 3,850 years have passed since that time and 1922; and in the year 1922 there were on the earth 15,393,815 Jews, according to the Jewish Year Book. The two people, then, had to double their numbers nearly 24 times in order to reach that number; or, if you please, double their population once in every 161 years, and a fraction.

By comparing the growth of the Jewish race with that of the Gentile, it is found that the Jews are a bit more prolific, and that it would require for Gentile doubling 168 3/10 years instead.

Now apply this to the earth's population and stand amazed at the mathematical testimony!

In the 5,077 years since Noah's marriage, starting with the two people originally, and doubling the number every 168 3/10 years, we would have 2 raised to the 30¾ power ending with 1922; and, lo, your population at that time should have been about 1,804,187,000 people, or practically exactly what was then found upon the earth.

Had not the Flood taken place you would have to reckon 2 raised to the 43rd power to cover the 7,000 years since Adam, and the population of the earth, instead of being 1,804,187,000, would now be 29,-559,799,808,000 or so great that the earth could not sustain any considerable proportion of them.

Lest somebody should object to the calculations of Williams, I bring you a page out of "Readings in Sociology" by Wilson D. Wallis, Professor of Anthropology and Sociology at the University of Minnesota, and Malcolm M. Willey, Professor of Sociology in the same University. This you will find on pages 264 and 265. · It is a forecast first for the future population of the world. They reckon 1% increase per year, which you will notice is a higher rate than the German Scientists carefully proved. They tell us that in 1928 there were 1,950,000,000 on earth, and they claim that in the year 2000 there will be 3,992,000,000, and in the year 2100 there will be 10,796,000,000.

If, therefore, their wild guesses that man has been on the earth for two millions of years, or even 100,000 years, or even 10,000 years, were true by a mathematical preci-

19

sion the population of the earth at the present time would be so big that the sun and its every satellite would be required to give them standing room.

To illustrate this, let me take a little further testimony from the text book of these same gentlemen. Their calculation per square mile for the United States at the present rate of increase is this:

The year 1930—62 people
The year 1950—151 people
The year 2000—665 people
The year 2100—12,983 people

The year 2200—mark you only two centuries and 68 years hence, the population per square mile, would be—253,348 people. Then they add this wise note:

"By changes in the standard of living, however, by improvements in the food supply, and by better economics generally, the density of 65 per square mile can greatly be exceeded; but the figures for the year 2000 and later are, of course, hopelessly impossible."

In other words, they want us to believe that the race for the last 100,000 years, the shortest period suggested by any of them for man's occupation of the earth, has grown so slowly that it only doubled once in 1612 51/100 years; an estimate which, if applied to the increase of Jews, would give us less than 5 on the face of the earth now; and yet in the next 268 years it will grow so fast as to give us about 4,087 times the world's present population.

That, mark you, in the face of known Scientific fact, that a race in its early history grows with far greater rapidity than in its later history, due to the circumstance that increased population multiplies necessities, increases diseases, brings about wars, emphasizes pestilence, increases famine; in fact, every enemy of man himself, not only keeps up with, but outruns the growth in population.

Now if these figures, following as they do, facts on the confession of the proponents of Evolution, do not shame them from their philosophy, then let it be understood that they are "joined to their idol," and there is nothing to do for their delusion, save to leave them alone.

However, be assured of this,—the future will reveal

### The Truth Triumphant

The Bible is an old Book, but it is not a discredited one. Its every single statement becomes clearer truth as the mists lift and men learn the facts.

In previous discourses I have called attention to the scientific accuracy of every verse in Genesis 1: but I possibly omitted to speak of that wonderful phrase, *"God made two great lights; the greater light to rule the day, and the lesser light to rule the night."*

For thousands of years after this was written, the Greeks were contending that the moon was much larger than the sun but because of its remoter distance less luminous. Modern Science again justified Moses.

In passing, let me call attention to another point which Modern Science is just now also doing.—Speaking of the Antediluvian civilization Moses writes, *"There were giants in the earth in those days."* Gen. 6: 4.

Take the much paraded Cro-Magnon race. In frame and brain capacity they were giants. Professor Conklin, writing of this man, says, "Since him there has been no marked increase in man's cranial capacity, and probably very little, if any, in his intellectual ability." The young men are reported to have been 6 feet 1½ inches, and the older men among them 6 feet 4½ inches.

You will remember, some of you, that in the letter I read to you last Sunday night

22

written by a young woman who is just taking her Ph.D. at the University of Minnesota, she asked, in a somewhat supercilious tone, "I suppose you do not even believe in the present progress of man?" and then answered her own question, "Some people are marking none."—evidently a gentle hint of the static state of mind on the part of the speaker! I prefer to let the Evolutionists themselves answer this question, and I bring forward one of their general favorites for this reply.

It can be found in "The Direction of Human Evolution" by Prof. Edwin Grant Conklin, who says, "There can be no doubt that human evolution has halted, either temporarily or permanently, and when we consider the fact that in every line of evolution progress is most rapid at first and then slows down until it stops, we cannot avoid the suspicion that in those lines in which human evolution has gone farthest and fastest it has practically come to an end. At least we may affirm that there is no prospect that the hand, the eye, or the brain of man will ever be much more complex or perfect than at present."

Further,

"It is the opinion of those who have studied the subject most that no modern race of men is the equal intellectually of the ancient Greek race. There has been no notable progress in the intellectual capacity of man in the past two or three thousand years, and it seems probable that the limits of intellectual evolution have been reached in the greatest minds of the race."

We agree absolutely with Prof. Conklin in this matter, only we cannot understand why he should stop with the Grecians. If he pushed back to the Jews he would find equal occasion for his remark, and in fact Moses would be a far better illustration of his contention than are the names of Socrates, Plato, and Aristotle.

The simple truth seems to be that man began on a higher plane than he has been able to maintain.

Sin is not helpful to a sound mind, nor does it make desirable contribution to a sound body; and the effect of sin upon the race for the 7000 years of its known history, Evolutionists refuse to reckon. History, however, does not, and cannot, disregard its essential element in human deterioration.

### THE FAITH OF BELIEVERS RESTS ON FACTS—NOT FICTION

Take the single illustration! David wrote, *"I will praise thee; for I am fearfully and wonderfully made: marvellous are thy works; and that my soul knoweth right well."* Ps. 139: 14.

Test out that single statement by the teachings of Science, and tell me if it be not so.

Quoting from medical authorities, one writes: "There are in the human body 600 muscles, 1000 miles of blood vessels, and 550 arteries important enough to name. The skin, spread out, would cover 16 square feet. It has 1,500,000 sweat glands which spread out on one surface, would occupy 10,000 sq. ft., and would cover 5 city lots, 20x100 ft. The lungs are composed of 700,000,000 cells, all of which we use in breathing,—equal to a flat surface of 2,000 square feet, which would cover a city lot. In 70 years, the heart beats 2,500,000,000 times, and lifts 500,000 tons of blood. The nervous system, controlled by the brain has 3,000,000,000,000 nerve cells, 9,200,000,000 of which are in the cortex or covering of the brain alone. In the blood are 30,000,000 white corpuscles, and 180,000,000,000,000 red ones. It is easy also to believe that the 'very hairs' of our heads are numbered—about 250,000."

Can anything be more pathetic than for some young Freshman, created of God, in such intricacy and with such infinite wisdom, to spew his infidelity into the face of the very God who created him; who saw his substance before it was in existence, and who wrote down in His book all his members and fashioned them when as yet there was none of them!

What a contrast such an infidel is with the mighty David, with his keen intellect and his accomplished scholarship, and who, in contemplating his own physical frame, gave God the glory, saying, *"How precious also are thy thoughts unto me, O God! how great is the sum of them!"* Ps. 139: 17.

## However, the Future of Christianity Is as Safe as Sound

Cain rejected the blood thereof, and carried forth from the presence of the Lord the mark of judgment. The Antediluvians grieved the Holy Ghost, but endured the judgment that buried them out of sight forever; but neither was the atoning blood set aside because Cain rejected it, nor the proffered salvation refused to Noah and his house because Antediluvians laughed at it.

When Frances E. Clark, known as "Father Clark" of the World's Christian Endeavor Society, was yet alive, he said, "The Darwinian theory, whatever it may be called today, has doubtless unsettled many

26

minds. A hazy agnosticism has often taken the place of strenuous belief."

Thank God, those who accept the Scriptures are not left to find their way through fog banks; for them the sun shines, and the pathway of life is plain. Or, if we change the figure a bit, and think of ourselves as crossing the Sea of Time, *"we have a strong consolation who have fled for refuge, to lay hold of the Hope set before us, which Hope we have as an anchor of the soul, both sure and steadfast, and which entereth into that within the veil."* Heb. 6: 18-19.

The story is told of how down at Gloucester, Mass., a ship was wrecked, and the wounded were brought ashore. Among them was an old sailor who was so badly hurt that little hope of his living could be entertained. His comrades came in to the fishing house and gathered about his bed and waited for the opinion of the physician called. He felt his pulse, took his temperature, and then he said, "He will not live long." The sailor was out of his mind, rambling in his conversation, of sea and storm, but after a while he quieted and seemed to sleep. The hour for the medicine came on, and one of his fellow sailors raised him up and said, "Mate, how are you now?" With a smile he looked into the eye of his friend, and answered, "All right; my anchor holds,"—and he was gone.

That is the Faith we preach! Christ, the Anchor of the soul! The antidote to infidelity; the personal ground of Faith.

*"He that believeth on Him hath eternal life, and shall not come into condemnation but is passed out of death into life."*

# "Ten Burning Questions"

This Volume from the pen of the author, W. B. Riley, and the Fleming H. Revell Press, contains the following vital themes:—

1. "Is the Bible a Human or a Divine Book?"
2. "The Old Versus the New Faith, or Why Fundamentalism?"
3. "Shall It Be Theological Liberty or License?"
4. "What of the Church After Nineteen Hundred Years?"
5. "Humanism—Is It Also and Only Heathenism?"
6. "Is Twentieth Century Society Rotting?"
7. "Shall the United States Re-Enthrone King Barleycorn?"
8. "Shall Affinities and Free Love Displace the Family?"
9. "Shall It Be Christianity or Communism?"
10. "Are World Governments Doomed? What Redemption?"

# EVOLUTION

The author has published several volumes upon this general subject. Conspicuous among these is his volume "Inspiration or Evolution" 12 chapters, 271 pages, second edition. Arranged in such a form as to be used in Polemics classes in Colleges, Bible Schools and Theological Seminaries. Subjects treated:—

1. The Bible—Is It an Evolution or an Inspiration?
2. The Theory of Evolution—Does it Tend to Atheism?
3. The Theory of Evolution—Does it Tend to Anarchy?
4. Civilization—Is it an Evolution? Christian Fundamentals in School and Church;
   Apr¹-June, 1924.
5. Evolution or Sovietizing the State through its Schools.
6. Shall We Longer Tolerate the Teaching of Evolution?
7. The Conflict of Christianity with Its Counterfeit.
8. Corporate Control—The Peril of Christian Education.
9. The Present Crisis in the Professing Church.
10. A Skeptic's Philosophy and the Second Coming.
11. Prophecy and the Approaching Kingdom.
12. Modernism—or the Challenge of Orthodoxy.

# The Northwestern Bible and Missionary Training School

This School was founded Oct. 2, 1902 by the author. It commenced with a day class of 7 students. 30 years later it enrolled 437 students. It graduates are in every country, and hundreds of them are pastors, evangelists and Christian workers in America.

It has a 2-year course for College and University graduates; 3-year course for High School graduates, and a 4-year course for those who have not had the High School training.

Its curriculum is conceded to be one of the highest.

Its graduates are in great demand. Its Tuition, Board and Room are exceedingly reasonable.

For a catalogue or any information, and for application blank write to the Northwestern Bible and Missionary Training School, 20 S. 11th St., Minneapolis, Minn.

### 10c Booklets

The Church After 1900 Years

The Challenge of Orthodoxy

Bryan, the Great Commoner and Christian

Christ and His City

Will Christ Come Again?

"Evolution—a False Philosophy"

Evolution — Mathematically Disproved.

Shall We Longer Tolerate the Teaching of Evolution?

The Eclipse of Faith

Fundamentalism—What Is It?

The Scientific Accuracy of the Sacred Scriptures

The Interchurch, or the Kingdom by Violence

Redemption of the Downtown

Theological Liberty vs. License of Infidelity

Socialism in Our Schools

Is Society Rotting?

*All 16 Booklets to One Order, $1.00.*

### Order from
## L. W. CAMP
#### 1020 Harmon Place
#### Minneapolis, Minnesota

# THE
# THEORY OF EVOLUTION--
# DOES IT TEND
## TO ATHEISM?

By

W. B. RILEY, D.D.

Minneapolis, Minn.

All rights reserved by the Author.

# BOOKS BY DR. W. B. RILEY

| | |
|---|---|
| GOD HATH SPOKEN .................... | $1.75 |
| (Report of Christian Fundamentals Convention—1919.) | |
| EVOLUTION OF THE KINGDOM, Revised Edition, paper 75c, cloth ............... | 1.50 |
| THE PERENNIAL REVIVAL, cloth ....... | 1.25 |
| THE CRISIS OF THE CHURCH, cloth ..... | 1.25 |
| THE MENACE OF MODERNISM, paper 50c, cloth ..................................... | |
| EPHESIANS, The Three-Fold Epistle, paper 40c, cloth ....................... | 1.00 |
| MESSAGES FOR THE METROPOLIS ..... | 1.00 |
| Old Testament Types, paper ............ | .40 |
| The Gospel in Jonah, paper ............. | .25 |
| Daniel vs. Darwinism, paper ............ | .25 |
| Modern Amusements .................... | .15 |
| Jerusalem and the Jew ................. | .10 |
| The Challenge of Orthodoxy ........... | .10 |
| The Scientific Accuracy of the Scriptures .. | .10 |
| Modernism in Baptist Schools ........... | .10 |
| The Great Question, Who Was Christ? .... | .10 |
| The Eclipse of faith ..................... | .10 |
| Christian Science and Divine Healing ...... | .10 |
| The Interchurch, or The Kingdom by Violence .................................. | .10 |
| The Gospel for War Times .............. | .10 |
| Spiritualism, or Can We Commune With the Dead? ................................ | .15 |
| Theory of Evolution, Is It Unscientific and Unscriptural? ........................... | .10 |
| Theory of Evolution Does it Tend to Atheism? .................................. | .10 |
| Speaking With Tongues .................. | .05 |
| Redemption of The Downtown .......... | .10 |
| Conflict of Christianity With Its Counterfeit ..................................... | .10 |
| Prof. Kent, or Cutting the Heart Out of the Bible ................................ | |
| The Bible—Is It an Evolution or an Inspiration? ............................ | .10 |

Order From

**L. W. CAMP**

1006 Harmon Place,            Minneapolis, Minn.

# THE THEORY OF EVOLUTION—
## DOES IT TEND TO ATHEISM?

"The wicked, thru the pride of his countenance, will not seek after God. God is not in all his thoughts." Psa. 10:4.

THE custom of selecting severe texts with which to sting one's intellectual opponents, is hardly praiseworthy, if even it be pardonable. I should treat this text with more pleasure if it did not open with the words **"the wicked"**, since I am not at all disposed to bring any moral railing against the men whose "new" religion is so plain a departure from the old paths, but not believing in the right of the individual to either make Scripture to suit himself or even change it into acceptable terms, I must take the text as I find it and treat it in the light of our theme—"The Theory of Evolution, Does It Tend to Atheism?"

The reasons for its selection will appear as we progress with this discussion. Beyond doubt, the intelligent traveler takes note, not alone of the character of the path his feet may be treading, but inquires deliberately "Whith-

I was lost once in the deep woods of northern Minnesota. I spent weary hours in a footsore journey; groped my way thru the blackest night I have ever known, and faced all the

3

while the fury of storm and rain, and it all came about in consequence of taking a path that looked attractive but led me astray. This experience is a parable and raises the question, "Whither does this evolutionary path tend?"

Turning back to the text and ignoring its opening indictment, I call attention to the points of parallelism between the remaining portions and that now popular theory known as Evolution. There are three: Pride of Intellect; Practical Irreligion, and Potential Atheism.

## PRIDE OF INTELLECT

"The wicked thru the pride of his countenance". The word "countenance" here refers not so much to the pride some people have in beholding themselves in a mirror, as it suggests and symbolizes self-esteem. Jos. Parker says, "It refers literally to the heightening of the nostril, the lifting of the head".

In the study of this suggestion, therefore, three important points, at which the pride of intellect now expresses itself.

1. **This century is seeing a revival of the original temptation.** When Satan tempted our first mother to disobedience, he did it by the subtle promise of "wisdom". "Then your eyes shall be opened and ye shall be as gods, knowing good and evil; and when the woman saw that it was a tree to be desired to make one wise, she took of the fruit thereof and did eat". Beyond all doubt, there is a progress in the temptation recorded in Gen-

esis. The first appeal was to the lust of the flesh, "good for food"; the second to the lust of the eye, "pleasant to the eyes"; the third to the pride of life, "a tree to be desired to make one wise", and it was at this third point that Satan reached the acme of his machinations! Great as is the temptation in the lust of the flesh, subtle as is the entreaty of pleasure for the eye, more powerful still is the appeal in the prospect of wisdom!

Each century in turn adopts a shibboleth and yields willing obedience to the ideal thereby expressed. The Twentieth Century has chosen **"Scholarship"** and that word has become both its religion and its god. In Germany they may name it "Kultur"; in England they may call it "Science"; in America they may phrase it "Scholarship", but in each country it represents the same claim, namely, "Wisdom is with **us**"!

This conceit is described by one writer as a result of the invention "of certain mechanical contrivances for abolishing time and space" and "expresses an inordinate but unjustifiable vanity". Practically every book now written by a modernist is big with such phrases as "The sure results of science", "The scholarship of the century", "The intellectual attainments of the times", "the fine products of university education", "the wondrous wisdom of these days", etc. It is a contagious claim and intellectually anemic men are particularly subject to the infection. One sound reason for the most thoro education exists at this point. Men of mediocre endowment, or only partial

5

training are particularly tempted at this point! This accounts for the false claims of classical learning where little or none of the same exists; the frenzied endeavor to secure literary degrees where no merit warrants the granting of the same, the keen candidacy for college and university professorships without peculiar fitness, and the impetuous rush to the printing press with every immature or amateur expression of thought! Satan has again triumphed and has taken us with ease by the hint "Be wise"!

**2. Science is now the subtle word of Satanic employment.** It is a word that expresses the idea "I know" and so sums up in a single term the conceit of the age. To immature minds, Science, as now employed, seems to be synonymous with Omniscience. To call a thing "scientific" is, in the judgment of such deceived ones, to establish it forever. That may account for the fact that we no longer have books on Biology, on History, on Philosophy, on Religion, but we are taught "the Science of Biology," "the Science of History," "the Science of Philosophy," "the Science of Religion," and we have so far converted this word into a mere mental commodity that a designing woman employs it for purely commercial purposes by calling her mental writings "Christian Science", and multitudes are deceived thereby.

We have had books written recently on "The Descent of Man". We are sadly in need of a volume on "The Degradation of Words", and

6

central in that discussion would be the strange and unjustifiable uses to which this word "Science" is now being subjected. O! Great and good word! but so bandied about by designing men as to be, like its Master, marred past recognition. What crimes against intelligence are committed in thy name Oh Science! This also is Satan's work!

The prospect of becoming gods is still a potent appeal. "Ye shall be as gods". No wonder our first mother went down before it! No wonder our first father fell for it! Nor is it any wonder their children, (born not only in this sin but of it), should surrender at the same point.

I was present a few days since in an evangelical ministers' meeting, and heard a man decry the old philosophy that we are "sinners" as an idea wholly out of date, and as most unworthy our matchless, manly dignity. To his brethren he said, "We are gods! Let us not forget the great apostle's teaching, 'Ye also are His offspring;' forasmuch then as we are the offspring of God, we ought not to talk continuously in the terms of humility, but rather in those of self-appreciation and praise"!

The speaker evidently forgot two things; that Paul was quoting from heathen poets when he made that declaration; and second, that when certain men at Lystra, seeing a miracle wrought at his hands upon an impotent one, brought oxen and garlands and would have done sacrifice to Barnabas as Jupiter and

7

Paul as Mercury, they rent their clothes and ran in among the people, crying out "Why do ye these things? We are also men of like passions with you and preach unto you that ye should turn from these vanities unto the living God who made heaven and earth and the sea and all that in them is". (Acts 14:11-15.)

A few years since, when Reginald Campbell attained the zenith of public attention by the explosion of his own faith, we paid much to what he had to say; now that he has fallen back to the nadir of obscurity we are like to forget his pretentious claims, "My God is my deeper self"!

Nietzsche, who in the judgment of Prof. Williams of Oxford, was the greatest exponent of evolution known to the age, said "Egoism is the prime characteristic of the noble soul"! If the Pharisee of the New Testament who went into the Temple to pray, were alive now, he would receive the commendation of all evolutionists and be an accepted leader among the "New Theologians". The superman, prophesied by so-called modern science, is nothing more nor less than a repetition of Satan's garden triumph; and again the sons of Adam are delighting themselves in the taste of forbidden fruit", tempted to it by the lie, "Ye shall be as gods".

Passing from the first sentence of the text to the second, we go from cause to effect. It may be properly phrased

8

## PRACTICAL IRRELIGION.

"He will not seek God"! The whole tendency of evolution takes one away from faith in God and in the end, even denies the fact of God.

1. **The theory proposes to explain all things apart from God.** Henry Van Dyke, in "The Gospel for an Age of Doubt", institutes a comparison between the genealogy of man as recorded in Luke's gospel, and that created by evolution. He admits having reduced Lyman Abbott's description of the descent, but says "I have retained its every essential" and then recites: "Monera began Amoebae, Amoebae began Synamoebae; Synamoebae, began Ciliated Larve; Ciliated Larva began primeval Stomach Animals; Primeval Stomach Animals begat Gliding Worms; Gliding Worms begat Soft Worms; Soft Worms begat Sack Worms; Sack Worms begat Skull-less Animals; Skull-less Animals begat Single-Nostrilled Animals: Single Nostrilled Animals Begat Primeval Fish; Primeval Fish begat Mud Fish; Mud Fish begat Gilled Amphibians; Gilled Amphibians begat Tailed Amphibians; Tailed Amphibians begat Primeval Amniota; Primeval Amniota begat Primary Mammals; Primary Mammals begat Pouched Animals; Pouched Animals begat Semi-apes; Semi-apes begat Tailed apes; Tailed apes begat Man-like apes; Man-like Apes begat Ape-like men; Ape-like Men begat Men". And now the Dean of a Divinity School completes the chain by "the inclusion of Jesus"!

9

I do not wonder that you smile, nor yet that you hold such a suggestion in ridicule and contempt, but I ask you to pause before it long enough to compare it with the origin of man as recorded in the Blessed Book. "And Jesus himself began to be about thirty years of age, being (as was supposed) the son of Joseph, which was the son of Heli, which was the son of Matthat, which was the son of Levi * * * which was the son of Nathan, which was the son of David which was the son of Jesse, which was the son of Obed, which was the son of Boaz, which was the son of Salmon, * * * * which was the son of Phares, which was the son of Judah, which was the son of Jacob, which was the son of Isaac, which was the son of Abraham, which was the son of Thara, which was the son of Nachor * * * * which was the son of Arphaxad, which was the son of Sem, which was the son of Noe, which was the son of Lamech, which was the son of Mathusala, which was the son of Enoch, which was the son of Jared, which was the son of Maleleel, which was the son of Cainan, which was the son of Enos, which was the son of Seth, which was the son of Adam, which was the son of God". (Luke 3:23-38.)

The first of these trees makes man the product of a blind force, named "spontaneous generation" and gives him an animal ancestry; the second makes him the creature and child of The Most High. Without now attempting to settle which is the saner expression, or which holds the more certain truth, I cite them to prove the absolute correctness of the text, namely The evolutionist will not acknowledge God!

2. **The appeal of evolution is to worship creation vs. the Creator.** Kant, whose philosophy conformed with the Darwin theory, acknowledged no allegiance to personal Creator, but confessed that he felt "a reverence approaching worship" for "the starry heavens above" and "the inner consciousness of man", or in other words, for the creation and creature, but none whatever for the Creator. In fact the existence of a Creator is practically denied. "Science is everywhere using impersonal ideas in explaining the universe" * *. "The idea of creation has been merged in the vaguer conceptions of evolution", says Gerald Birney Smith, the evolutionist professor of Chicago University.

Once more the "modernist" has returned to the old pagan pantheism, and speaks of God as "a spirit working within the cosmos". Prof. McGiffert and other evolutionists, tell us that "the divine is no more separate and aloof. It is within and organic with the human", and further remark, "God is considered as the soul of the world; the spirit animating nature; the universal force which takes the myriad forms of heat, light, gravity, electricity and the like". Therefore, these men are correct, the ancient then who worshipped the sun, moon and stars really bowed before the only god, and for that matter, the modern heathen who worships wood, stones and even serpents is still worshipping some expression of the only god there is. To say that such a god is not the God of the Christian, and that he is thoroly unknown to Biblical conceptions, is to state a spiritual axiom.

3. **The evolution-propaganda promotes both these procedures.** To the evolutionist, Christianity is little more sacred than any ancient Greek cult. Matthew Arnold, while professing to find in Christ "the Light of World," was a modernist with all its implications, and in one of his poems he writes:

> "Forgive me, masters of the mind,
> At whose behest I long ago
> So much unlearned, so much resigned;
> I come not here to be your foe;
> I seek these anchorites, not in ruth,
> To curse and to deny your truth;
>
> Not as their friend, or child, I speak,
> But as on some far northern strand,
> Thinking of his own gods, a Greek,
> In pity and mournful awe might stand
> Before a fallen Runic stone,—
>
> For both were faiths, and both are gone".

What then is the conclusion of the whole matter, other than that which is expressed in the last sentence of our text—

## POTENTIAL ATHEISM?

"God is not in all their thoughts."

1. **The greater exponents of evolution have been unbelievers.** If we thought anyone would attempt to debate this we would call the roll, quote from their writings and prove the statement. I am not saying these men have

no god; I am saying that few of them recognize the God of the Bible, or regard the teachings of that Book as final and authoritative.

They might resent being called "atheists" but under the most favorable conditions could not claim to be Christian believers. One wonders if that is not a prime reason why their so-called sciences remain mere speculations, hypotheses, theories, and no more. One cannot escape the conviction that no man can come into any light who does not walk in His light and in the light of the Word. Has it ever occurred to you that all the fixed sciences, about which men no longer debate, were discovered and proven and exploited by believers? The Copernican theory of the Universe is no longer a controversy, but Copernicus, while a Papist, was an ardent believer in both God and His book, and the very breath of his childhood was that of the bishop's house. Kepler, in his early days, was a theological student whose scientific tendencies and attainments triumphed over his gospel ministry, but were exercised in the same unfaltering faith and Kepler found in Science the thoughts of God. Galileo, the father of physics, while suffering from the church, remained faithful, as he believed, to the God of the Bible and the Bible of God. Sir Isaac Newton, whose theories were long since changed into certainties, was the stepson of a preacher and a patron of the faith once for all delivered. Henry Van Dyke says, "We observe in those departments of science where the knowledge of the magnitude and splendid order of the physical universe is most clear and exact, the most illustrious men have not been skeptics but sincere and steadfast believers" and then he gives a list of the most brilliant mathematicians ever assembled, and says they were believers, every one.

I am inclined to think that their Science was accurate because they were believers. "The light is with Him". How strange that not were established sciences discovered every by believers but even the opinions of such later believers, working in the scientific realm, as Sir James and Alexander Simpson, George Stokes, Lord Kelvin, Pasteur, and their like, when contrasted with the pure suppositions and speculations of a sceptical Darwin, a doubting La Marcke, an unbelieving Spencer, an agnostic Huxley, monist Haeckel, and a rationalist Weismann, are comparative certainties. At this moment Mendelism gives every promise of proving its contentions and forcing science to accept the creative theory of Genesis—"to each seed it is given to bring forth after its kind", and Gregor Mendel was a godly monk.

**2. Converts to the theory of evolution are almost without exception destructive critics.** Those ministers who have received this Darwinian supposition and dared to believe a science, make up today a school of men not only disturb the churches of God papist and evangelical alike, but are the very men who are denying the veracity of the Book, disputing the Virgin Birth and Deity of Jesus, demanding that God be no longer an autocrat, but accept His position in a democracy—in fact, practically attempting His dethronement. When they become professors in universities and theological seminaries, their influence is a bitter fruit. O. B. Server, in "The Bible Champion" cites many instances in proof of this position. In one theological seminary a certain young student had invited ten of his fellows to come to his room for a prayer meeting. Not one of them accepted, and the last one exclaimed, "Pray? I haven't anyone to pray to! Those who have quit these seminaries and at the same time disclaimed their call to preach, and deliberately accepted other callings or professions are a legion and in every instance it was due to what they received from instructors, who were Darwin devotees.

My own associate in the ministry was in a class of sixteen. He sat at the feet of Prof. Douglas MacIntosh, now famed as a Yale theological professor, and widely known as a "new" theologian and evolutionist. Eight of the sixteen accepted his evolutionary hypothesis and went with him the length of all its conclusions. The entire eight left the ministry. The other eight of the class repudiated it, and that half now represent an effective preaching force.

It is reported (on one of our mission fields,) a Union Christian College (so-called) sent out twenty six graduates. One of them went into the ministry and twenty five relapsed into the dark unfaith of heathenism.

A young woman teacher in the public schools and a valued church worker, went to Chicago University to study to fit herself for her vocation. That was the end of her church usefulness, and Mr. Server says, "She seemed to have attended a slaughter house of faith and a morgue of piety".

I could, out of personal observation, cite scores of instances, met in my travels across the continent, of young men who have tearfully reported to me the waning of their faith and the wreck of their ministry thru the acceptance of the evolutionary theory. Is it any wonder when their theological professors, following this philosophy, have affirmed in their presence "In the light of our comparative historical study, any claim to exclusiveness and incomparableness on the part of Christianity, as a positive religion, must be entirely abandoned"?

Some of these instructors have sought to quiet the fears and assuage the griefs of parents, bereft by the unbelief of their children, saying, "We teach here theistic evolution"! It is a poor sop "which", as Prof. George McCready Price justly says, "is in its essential nature as thoroly pagan or heathen as anything that ever grew up in Greece or India".

Then let us come to the conclusion of the whole matter.

3. **The entire tendency of this theory is to atheism.** Multitudes of its followers will not admit so much. They maintain they have a god. Possibly; the god of a Huxley,—unknown

and unknowable. Possibly; the god of Haeckel and insentient force, unconsciously framing and finishing. Possibly; the god of a Coe, a Rauschenbusch, a Frank Crane,—who has played the aristocrat long enough and must now descend to his proper place "in a democracy"; but to this whole company, the God of the Bible is unknown. "He is not in all their thoughts", and their attempt to rule Him is no longer even disguised.

On their own confession, the authority of our faith has perished, and the sacred convictions of past centuries have been swept forever away. They no longer believe in our God; they no longer believe in an infallible Bible; they no longer believe in the Virgin Birth of Christ or any other essential feature of His deity; they hold to ridicule the personality and power of the Holy Ghost; they define regeneration as "adolescence"; they reduce evangelization to "social uplift"; they think of mission work in terms of "international commerce" and "educational opportunity"; they look upon the church as a mere medium of financing their evolutionary program! The sacred codes of Scripture are to them only social conceptions strengthened by some centuries of practice; marriage is a domestic convenience, but holds no moral obligations; the Sabbath is little less than a social nuisance, and sobriety, imposed by law, violates every principle of that progressive theory "The survival of the fittest".

What will be the final result? You say, "No man can forecast it". Any intelligent man can rehearse it. There is nothing new under the sun. 150 years ago France disposed of the true church, massacring Protestants in multitudes; 150 years ago France repudiated the Bible; 150 years ago France dethroned God and inpersonating Human Reason, Liberty, Equality and Fraternity, in a street strumpet, rid itself of all the restraints with which the Bible had ever sought to bind it. Then what? Then, as one has said, "Her flourishing manufacturing cities fell into decay; her fertile districts returned to native wildness; a period of moral and intellectual decadence ensued, and the whole nation plunged by a swift descent to the bloody abyss of the revolution by the way of anarchy, ruin and the Reign of Terror".

Think you it will be different this time? I tell you, Nay! The doctrine of Charles Darwin, in proportion as it dominates the future, the biological theory of evolution to the extent of its final acceptance, will make the recent baptism of blood, brought on by Nietzsche and Treitschke under the domination of that biological theory, as compared with the baptism yet to come, as a local shower to the flood that will prevail over every mountain.

"The survival of the fittest" is a soft sounding phrase, but when it is interpreted in the light of "the struggle for existence", it becomes a startling menace. Fill a nation with the German conceit that "We are the superior race, and all the women of weaker nations are our natural prey, and the men of such nations our legitimate servants", and you turn the world into a slaughter house, and as one has said, "There is no logic to show why such a code of international ruffianism is wrong or at all blame-worthy if the evolution theory be true". Its premises granted, an Armageddon is the result. I am no alarmist, but I am not blind! The triumph of Darwinism will introduce the day of the Great Tribulation!

# THE THEORY OF EVOLUTION--
# DOES IT TEND TO ANARCHY?

By

### W. B. RILEY, D.D.
Minneapolis, Minn.

All rights reserved by the Author.

# BOOKS AND TRACTS ON TIMELY TOPICS

| | |
|---|---|
| God Hath Spoken | $1.75 |
| (200 pages of Addresses by the leading Bible expositors of the world. A text book on the Christian Fundamentals.) | |
| Evolution of the Kingdom, paper 75¢, cloth, | 1.50 |
| Perennial Revival, cloth, | 1.25 |
| Crisis of the Church, cloth, | 5 |
| Menace of Modernism, paper 50¢, cloth, | .:10 |
| Ephesians, paper 40¢, cloth, | 1.00 |
| Messages for the Metropolis, cloth, | 1.00 |
| Old Testament Types, paper, | .40 |
| The Gospel in Jonah, | .25 |
| Daniel vs. Darwinism, | .25 |
| Modern Amusements, | .15 |
| Spiritualism, or Can We Commune With the Dead? | .15 |
| Jerusalem and the Jew, | .10 |
| The Challenge of Orthodoxy, | .10 |
| Modernism in Baptist Schools, | .10 |
| The Great Question, | .10 |
| The Eclipse of Faith, | .10 |
| Christian Science and Divine Healing, | .10 |
| The Interchurch, or the Kingdom by Violence, | .10 |
| Redemption of the Downtown, | .10 |
| Speaking with Tongues, | )5 |

L. W. Camp
1006 Harmon Place    Minneapolis, Minn.

# THE THEORY OF EVOLUTION— DOES IT TEND TO ANARCHY?

2 Peter 2:1-22.

WITH this address we propose to conclude for the present the series upon Evolution, into which we were led in consequence of Prof. Kent's visit to Minneapolis.

The greatest single wonder of the Bible exists in the circumstances that it compasses every vital subject and when it finished with a theme, has spoken the sanest word that will ever be uttered concerning the same.

If Peter were a living prophet, we suspect that the followers of Darwin would complain of this chapter as too personal, since they are the very men who have "denied the Lord who bought them" and who have been "followed by a multitude", and "by reason of whom the way of truth is now evil spoken of", and "who, with well turned words, have made merchandise of the people". The result of this is fully set forth in verses that follow, to the end of the chapter, and considered together, they provide a basis for the discussion of our theme.

There are three statements regarding Evolution around which we propose to build this discourse; The Evolutionary Hypothesis is unproven; The Theory's Promises are Unfulfilled; and The Product of the Theory is Anarchy.

## 1. EVOLUTIONARY HYPOTHESIS IS UNPROVEN.

This is the charge of its opponents. It is a charge they will continue to make. In making

3

it, they know they are on absolutely safe grounds and they also know they are on scientific grounds. The attempt of Darwin devotees to make the appeal that every opponent of Evolution is opposing science would be pathetic if a stronger word were not needed to describe it. These Darwin disciples know full well no well-educated man ever opposes true science, or could by any conceivable debate be pushed into a position where he would ever appear to so do. Science, to us, is as safe as the Son of God, for it is simply His way of work, and "without Him was not anything made that was made". Kepler, the great Christian believer, cried upon certain scientific discoveries, "O, I think God's thought after Him" So does every true scientist. But the work of such men is something more than multiplied suppositions, palmed off in the name of Science, and then defended as I have demonstrated. The one effective appeal made to the great student body of America in this matter, rests upon an utter falsehood. It is most natural for young and inexperienced men and women to be ready to part company with those seniors, who are made to appear to oppose "search for truth". When the President of Dartmouth College intimates that orthodox men believe in anything less than science, and open-minded search for the truth, he states what every thoughtful man knows to be an utterly false charge, and when in defense of his position he quotes, "Ye shall know the truth and the truth shall make you free", he lays himself open to the indictment of false assumption,

4

since the man does not live who can declare the Evolutionary Theory to be true, and, at the same time, be himself speaking the truth! The man who opposes Darwinism cannot be indicted with opposing science!

**This is the confession of the Darwinian advocates.** We have been quoting from leading scientists to show that they either clearly admit no sufficient proofs of the Darwinian Theory, or openly oppose the same as utterly unscientific. We had used such names as Profs. Shaler and Everitt of Harvard, Lionel S. Beale of Kings College, London, Virchow of Berlin, Zoeckler of Griefswald, Fleischman of Erlangen, Dennart, Goette, Hoppe, Prof. Paulson of Berlin, and others. But to all of this the Evolutionists have answered, "They are men of ten years since. In that time our position has been shown to be scientific". Fortunately for the truth and unfortunately for this fallacious argument, Prof. William Bateson, the distinguished representative of Cambridge University, and confessedly the greatest living authority on the subject, now comes out in the great assembly of Scientists in Toronto and admits that discussions on Evolution are practically at an end; morphology, genetics have alike failed to yield any evidence. The changes once claimed were confessedly gratuitous. "Less and less was heard about evolution in genetical circles and now the topic was dropped. When a student in other sciences asks us what is now currently believed about the origin of species, we have no clear answer to give. Faith has given place to agnosticism". This is all the more remarkable a confession because made by a friend of the Evolutionary Theory, who had followed his speculations to the point of practical despair.

**This confession discredits both its scientific and social claims.** When the scientists come back from their research and admit "We have exhausted every clue and have found no proofs", what absurdity for small men to go as gaily on as tho they had both leaders and light. It is a fresh illustration of the parable of our Lord. It is the foolish man, building his house once more upon the sand, and that in spite of the certainty that rains will descend and floods will come and winds will blow and beat upon that house and it will fall and great will be the fall of it".

No conclusion can be correct when the premises are utterly false. All the beneficial results, promised by biological evolutionists, whether they were expected in the realm of plant life, animal life or human life, have excited only false hopes, and all expectations indulged as a consequence are doomed to disappointment. A lie, because you dress the same in the name of science, cannot produce desirable fruits. The philosophies of Hegel, Kant and Descartes were adopted by millions of men, but to this good hour not one blessed result has ever issued to the disciples of the same. The same principle will apply in Darwinism.

## ITS PROMISES ARE DESTINED NO FULFILMENT.

It promised social improvement and it has only produced social putridity. That is the thing of which Peter is speaking in this chapter. Edmond Kelly, himself a Socialist, declares, "Socialism is not anarchism, but order; not communism but justice. It doesn't propose to abolish competition but to regulate it; not to abolish property but to consecrate it; not to abolish the home but to make the home possible". Such would be an evolution worth while, but when or where has any man ever seen a result of Evolutionary Socialism as Kelly describes? More often the Michael Bakunin interpretation of Socialism has dominated. "Tear out of your hearts the belief in the existence of God. The first lie is God, the second lie is the idea of right. And when you have freed your minds of the fear of God and from the childish respect for right, then all the remaining chains that bind you, called civilization, property, marriage, morality, justice, will snap asunder like threads. Let your own happiness be your own law".

This is where Peter's words have their application. "Them that walk after the flesh in the lust of uncleanness and despise government. Presumptuous are they, self-willed, they are not afraid to speak evil of dignities. \*\*\* But these, as natural brute beasts, made to be taken and destroyed, speak evil of the things that they understand not, and shall utterly perish in their own corruption. \*\* Spots are they and blemishes, sporting themselves with their own deceivings while they feast with you; having eyes full of adultery and that cannot cease from sin; beguiling unstable souls; an heart they have exercised with covetous practices,

7

*197*

cursed children, which have forsaken the right way, and are gone astray, following the way of Balaam, who loved the wages of unrighteousness. These are wells without water, clouds that are carried with a tempest, to whom the mist of darkness is reserved forever. For when they speak great swelling words of vanity, they allure thru the lusts of the flesh, thru much wantonness, those that were clean escaped from them who live in error."

John Burroughs, the great naturalist, in a most informing article, published in the New York Times Current History, thinks that the Evolution Theory by "a long, slow and painful process, gives man his moral conscience, and his concepts of right and wrong, of truth and falsehood, justice and mercy; and that it amounted practically to a new birth, making the fittest to survive, and that thru it was modern salvation made possible." He argues, "Only by man subordinating the rule of might to the rule of right, fair dealing, the common weal, justice to the weak as well as to the strong, were the rights of states and organized governments possible".

But, we ask, what evidence there is that any of this ever came by the evolutionary process? I know the mountains of Kentucky at first hand, and have had a fair degree of familiarity with the mountaineers; the men among whom family feuds live and flourish. Very recently two parties to one of those famed feuds met in a Court Room where certain of their number were on trial for life, for having killed their opposing fellows. After some little time, they shook hands, wept on one another's shoulders, decided to bury the hatchet forever and go back to their homes to be law-abiding, peaceful citizens and recognize the brotherhood of man. Was that a result of a "long, slow and painful process of evolution?" Not for one minute! It came in consequence of a Judge's appeal, who, animated himself by the Spirit of Christ, laid His great principles before these contestants and argued them so eloquently as to convince criminals of their crime, sinners of their sin, and never has even the rudiments of civilization resulted from the theory of Evolution.

Just as grafting a crab-apple tree makes it possible for the tree to bring forth pippins, by the introduction of a new life, finding expression in a new fruit, so wherever civilization has been at all lifted, improved, finished, it has been done, not by the cultivation of the old life, but by the introduction of new principles that made for progress; by the reaching down of a hand from above that laid hold and lifted. Civilization is not a product of Evolution. Civilization, wherever it is worthy of the name, is a pure product of Christianity. Take Christianity out of your civilization now and you will fall back, by an irresistible law, known in the language of science as "Reversal to type", to pagan first, heathenism afterwards, and finally to primitive brutalities and bestial behaviors.

This is not only true in the social realm, but it is true in the realm of government as well.

**The Evolution Theory promises true gov-**

9

ernment, but eventuates in dethroning all government. Never since the world had a beginning has any proposition been more clearly demonstrated than this. Take the nations that have tried out evolutionary Socialism, and ask yourself today what one of them you would choose for a home. Into what one you could carry your family tonight and feel any safety for it? Under what one of them you wish to make the purchase of property and look to that government for protection? Within the borders of what one would you like to bring up your babes? Hardly in Russia, where property rights are not regarded; where marriages are made and dissolved at will; where children are carried to brightly illuminated school buildings and by senior associates are led thru the dance until the early hours of the morning, while miserable mothers wait outside and beg to have their children come home, but are not allowed to exercise any authority whatever over them until many mothers are now saying, "There are no longer any children in Russia; only vicious little brutes, whose talk is only of money and pleasure".

If therefore the present rulership in Russia is ruthless, what can possibly be the character of that civil government when these children have come to its supremacy?

**This theory promised personal liberty and produced social slavery.** Here again the language of Peter is *a propos*. "While they promise them liberty, they themselves are the servants of corruption". "For of whom a man is overcome, of the same is he brought in bondage".

Take Tolstoi as a pitiable instance of this outworking. No man was ever so keen for liberty for himself and his fellow citizens. He sacrificed everything in behalf of its possible experience for his people, and signally failed, because of the social fabric of which he found himself a part, and failed also because his own theories, when they had their chance, refused to work. Finally, in order to be able to longer live, he took single sentence from the lips of Jesus, "Resist not evil", and became an apostle of "Passive resistence", and even at that saw the social slavery of his own country and people increasing until he counted himself a helpless victim of the same, and quitting his own family and house, sought the forest in which to die. His final and fruitless protest against a system that he himself had done more to popularize than any living Russian, for Tolstoi was a fellow-teacher with Proudhon, declaring "Property signifies that which has been given to me, which belongs to me exclusively, with which I can always do anything I like; which no one can take away from me; which will remain with me to the end of my life, and precisely that which I am bound to use, increase and improve. Now there exists but one piece of such property for any man—himself"; following this philosophy to its natural conclusion, he disclaimed all property rights, refused his social standing, treated with contempt his hereditary titles, strove as seldom mortal man has ever striven, to extricate himself from state and social entanglements and after every turn found himself into a new social slavery that produced only bitterness, despair and death. "While they promise liberty, they themselves are the servants of corruption, for of whom a man is overcome, of the same is he brought into bondage".

More than once Tolstoi turned to Christ, but just as often he turned away from Him. He took from Jesus what would fit his philosophy and what did not fit it, he refused, giving additional emphasis to Peter's language, "For if they have escaped the pollutions of the w... thru the knowledge of the Lord and Savior Jesus Christ, they are again entangled therein, and overcome, the latter end is worse with them than the beginning; for it had been better for them not to have known the way of righteousness, than, after they have known it, to turn from the holy commandment delivered unto them". (Vss. 20-21.)

What I am saying is this, When Socialism has spoken its last word and the theory of Evolution has uttered its last promise, there is no prospect in either, apart from God and Christ. The sympathetic writer may say, of Evolutionary Socialism, that "it has altruism at the basis of its philosophy, economics and ethics, and that by its anxiety to uplift, it comes into harmony with all that Christianity professes; that the fundamental ideas of anarchy, justice, liberty and equality, are ideals that... Christian also professes to love and to se... but he ought to know that when he makes... further remark, "Such ideals were prominent in the legislation of Moses and in the teachings of Jesus", he has missed the mark. All such ideals were **born** in the legislation of Moses and **have their being** in the teaching of Jesus, and that anarchy that disposes of God and puts a blind Force in His stead, as evolution does, and of Jesus Christ, as God's very Son, making Him nothing more than the beast brought to higher perfection, and of the Bible, holding it to be only an evolution of man's religious desires and experiences, has never yet produced a civilization worthy of the name, nor resulted in anything else than brutal ruffianism and never will!

To use the language of the same writer, but in a righteous sense, "All such expectations are iridescent dreams, contradicted by all human experience up to this very hour".

Finally, let the full truth be known.

## THE PRODUCT OF THE EVOLUTION THEORY IS BESTIAL BOLSHEVISM!

**The theory itself lays emphasis upon man's bestiality.** To teach men they are brutes developed to higher form, and to bring them to be willing to claim kinship with the ape, is to belittle them in their own judgment. It cannot be otherwise. No man can have the same sense of dignity, once he is brought to believe he has come up from a lower form of life, that belongs, inherently, in the one who lets the Bible teach him the truth, namely that he is the highest product of the Divine wisdom and plan, and the perfection of all God's thought in perfecting and peopling a world. Peter never heard of Charles Darwin, but the Holy Spirit who indited his sentences knew perfectly well how to contrast angels who in their higher origin and fellowship with God the Father, brought no railing accusation against heavenly dignities, and man, claiming kinship with natural brute beasts who hesitates not to speak evil of the same, nor yet to despise government.

It is a significant thing when White, the Socialist preacher of New York, and the socialist graduate of a Darwinian and liberal theological seminary, declares that he got dynamite with which he hopes to destroy the present order from his instruction in the halls of the same. He is revealing one of the true danger points not only to America, nor yet to our democratic government, but to the cause of Christianity itself—the Evolution Seminary!

**This whole vulgar theory tempts the virtuous to fresh vulgarities.** The strangest of modern spectacles is the sight of capped and gowned men, drawing salaries from tax payers or benevolently inclined persons, turning people from the knowledge of the Lord and Savior Jesus Christ, to entangle them again in Hegelian, Marxian and Darwinian philosophies. The result of this we are beginning to see, and more of it we will face when the future has become the present. John Burroughs is a notable scientist, an ardent believer in Darwinism, and yet John Burroughs admits that the Germans, by the adoption of this very philosophy became a menace to the world. Of them he writes in perfect line with Darwin's philosophy which they adopted, of the "struggle for existence" and "the survival of the fittest", "They are the fittest to survive by reason of sheer power; they are the least fit by reason of sheer brutality—their reliance upon the predatory methods and the lower aims of earlier times. They have gone forth to battle in the spirit of their ancestral Huns, and in many ways in a worse spirit. *** Wreckers of cathedrals, destroyers of libraries, despoilers of cemeteries, slayers of old men and women and children and priests and nuns, barbarians by instinct, pirates and incendiaries by practice, terrorists by training, slaves by habit and bullies by profession, void of humility, void of spirituality, resourceful but not inventive, thoro but not original, docile as individuals but brazen and defiant as a nation—ravishing, maiming, poisoning, burning, suffocating, deporting, enslaving, murderers of the very soul of a people, so far as it is in their power—the rest of the world can live on terms of peace and goodwill with them only after they have drained to the dregs the bitter cup of military defeat".

It all comes to what, then? Namely this, that **That theory tends to send Society to the sow-wallow of sin.** Pardon the language, but I bring it from the Apostle Peter. "But it is happened unto them, according to the true proverb, The dog is turned to his own vomit again, and the sow that was washed to her wallowing in the mire". Vs. 22.

That is where your Bakunin philosophy comes in, dethroning God, denying the difference between right and wrong, destroying the family, leaving not an ark to rescue one atom of a world consecrated to destruction. Perhaps never, since the days when the flood fell upon the face of the earth, were there so many nations away from God as tonight, and beyond all question, the one philosophy that has derided the codes of morals and religion alike, that has decried the claims of Christ to deity and has abolished once and forever all external authorities, is the Evolution Theory.

When, therefore, men in society, march their way thru the world, kicking aside every single tenet of law, it will result in a godless w that will make unto itself graven images and by bowing itself to them, go back to the heathenism of the past; that will take the name of the Lord God in vain, for the purpose of showing their contempt of such a term; that will trample the Sabbath day under its feet in order to prove its disrespect for any expression of law; that will refuse honor to father and mother on the ground that the family is not a Divine institution and parenthood imposes no obligations; that will kill; that will commit adultery without conscience because the law against the same was only made sacred by Capitalism; that will steal without conviction of sin, since personal property rights were never sacred; and that will take from neighbor house or wife or servant or beast, if he be able, on the sole ground that "in the struggle for existence" only the stronger have rights that are to be regarded. Is Peter's lang too strong? Is there any longer any d as to the relation between Evolution and Anarchy?

# HITLERISM

## OR THE
## PHILOSOPHY OF EVOLUTION
## IN ACTION

### BY DR. W. B. RILEY

#### PSALM 94

THE imprecatory Psalms attain popularity whenever war stalks the world. Then their language takes on definite meaning, and David is not only understood, but also appreciated. One might easily imagine that this 94th Psalm was born since Hitler began his practice of mass-murder and oppression. There are, however, but few who realize that Hitlerism is nothing other than the philosophy of Evolution in action.

This sermon is presented for the express purpose of proving that proposition. I propose to present it under the themes: Evolution—English in Origination; German in Cultivation, and World-wide in Devastation.

#### EVOLUTION, ENGLISH IN ORIGINATION

*It was born of a young English theologue's brain.*

Those who take the pains to look up the history of Charles Darwin will find that as a youth he was a student for the ministry; but an opportunity came for him to make a voyage round the world on the "Beagle" and he accepted it. More than once on this trip he indulged in controversy with his shipmates on the subject of religion, and in his arguments constantly appealed to the teachings of Scripture. It was some fifteen years later before he abandoned his evangelical faith, and then he confessed to his friend Hooker that he felt as guilty as if he were committing a murder.

The theory of Evolution, then, did not originate with, was not even revived by, a scientist, or a man of mature intellectual attainment; but rather from the mind of a young student for the ministry.

*Its early broadcast was by English men.*

CHARLES DARWIN was born in 1809 at Shrewsbury, England; and Alfred Russell Wallace in 1823 at Ush, Monmouth.

In 1859 Darwin was fifty years of age, and Wallace was but thirty-six; and yet the man who had started his life as a ministerial student and the one who had commenced his professional career as a research scientist, reached common conclusions, and their papers were read at the same meeting of the Linnaean Society of London and published together in "TRANSACTIONS" 1858.

Having originated in England, it was natural that *Englishmen became its early proponents.*

Herbert Spencer, a contemporary and a somewhat noted English philosopher, became easily a leader in the advocacy of this philosophy. His "PRINCIPLES OF PSYCHOLOGY," published four years before Darwin's "ORIGIN OF SPECIES," took the form of a positive approval of the philosophy of Evolution; while his work, "A SYSTEM OF SYNTHETIC PHILOSOPHY," in 1860, was an earnest of "THE FACTORS OF ORGANIC EVOLUTION" of 1887.

From that day, England has provided constant and efficient advocates of the philosophy, Sir Arthur Keith being among the most notable of them, and yet, having as his confreres in the philosophy an ever-increasing company of so-called scientists, ranging all the way from such names as that of William Bateson—an eminent biologist—down to J. B. McCabe, a shallow agnostic.

But this philosophy, finding its rise in England, has, like the winged seed of a Canadian thistle, been carried to all parts of the world, and found in certain national atmospheres quick root and rapid growth.

## EVOLUTION OF GERMAN CULTIVATION

*It was an exotic in Germany!* But the dwarf philosophy born in England, proved a flowering plant when carried across the channel and over the Rhine.

However, it must be said in faithfulness to the German university professor-company, and even to their men worthy to be called great scientists, that they were not the ones to give it welcome.

RUDOLPH VIRCHOW, born just two years ahead of Alfred Russell Wallace, was a Prussian from Pomerania, but studied at Berlin; and later in his professorship there, became the noted pathologist of his day. In the realm of archeology he was equally distinguished.

In fact, he was in Germany what Saul was in Israel —head and shoulders above his fellow scientists. The Darwin doctrine he repudiated *in toto*.

His junior, Ernst Haeckel, the German zoologist and atheist, proved to be the leader of the lesser breed of atheist or monist Germans, who adopted the philosophy and sought to impose it upon the university students of their day.

*Among theological professors the philosophy found its early friends.*

The reason for that fact is not far to seek! Inflated with a sense of superiority the theologians inaugurated the theory of Higher Criticism, which called into question the claims of divine Revelation, and based that theory on the Darwin hypothesis. A land that prospered under the doctrines of Luther, the practice of Bible precepts and so enjoyed the favor of God, fell into the common experience of both individuals and nations, namely, imagining itself *"some great one."* And because the schools were found manned by superior professors, the world began to pay its tribute, in the form of students traveling from many countries to that center.

5

So, Germany, made great by the favor of God, forgot the source of its strength and began to trust in itself. Materialism triumphed, and the Darwin doctrine of Evolution flourished accordingly. The Standard Encyclopedia says,

"It was in Germany, beyond any other European country, that the impulse given by Darwin twenty years ago (now 50) to the theory of evolution influenced the whole tenor of philosophical opinion."

The moment theologians forget God and begin to question and contort His Word, the result becomes a matter of record; and the land of Luther, between the years of 1873 and 1879, a short period of six seasons, increased in crime from fifty to between two hundred and three hundred per cent, while imprisonments in Prussia, Hanover and the Rhine provinces rose with an equal rapidity. Forty years ago, when the Darwin doctrine had reached its greatest popularity in that land, Dr. Bauer, one of the Imperial chaplains, preaching before the emperor himself, said,

"Affection, faith and obedience to the Word of God are unknown in this country, in this our great German Fatherland, which formerly was justly called 'the home of the faith.'" "On the contrary, it really seems as if it were the father of all lies who is now worshiped in Prussia." "Marriages are concluded without the blessing of the Church." "We still have a Sunday, but it is only a Sunday in name," and "now the servants of God are daily insulted."

About the same time a German correspondent of a London paper declared that in "Berlin house to house inquiry showed that in only one house in eight was there any regular use, or even possession, of the Bible; and this correspondent added, "The social deterioration in Germany and increase of crime does not come from ignorance. Nor does the presence of immorality arise from a lack of artistic and esthetic culture. Nor is intemperance the cause! The one chief reason for the degeneration of this once noble people is the *substitution of skepticism for faith in the Scriptures.*"

6

A shrewd observer remarked of Germany, "Ministers have lost their grip on the sword of the Spirit, have drifted into doubt and uncertainty; and the people, finding infidels positive and preachers insecure, have followed the men who seem to have convictions."

The Wellhausen School of Theology and the rise of Higher Criticism—indigenous to German soil—made the exchange of orthodoxy for the evolutionary hypothesis a natural barter by which not only the morals of the people were sabotaged, but Christianity itself was crucified afresh.

*From German universities this plague spread rapidly.*

Through the patronage of German universities by students from other nations, this German doubting became an epidemic and was carried to the many nations of the earth, menacing the respect of the Bible, the stability of morals, and even the progress of Christianity itself.

There are people, and not a few of them among the so-called intellectuals, who would prefer the cemetery to any position except "in the advance guard," and who adopt the latest philosophy as women indulge in painted nails or the spring style of hats! To show to what extremes a thing of this sort can go, take the survey of university shelves made in our own North America and reported by no less an authority than Dr. William Bell Dawson (Gold Medalist in Geology and Natural Science, and a Laureate of the Academy of Sciences, Paris) some years since. He said, "On the university shelves examined, we found in one library:

Books favorable to evolution, 83; opposed to evolution, 0;

Supporting atheistic evolution, 29; upholding theistic evolution, 3; non-committal, 51;

Discrediting the Divine inspiration of the Bible, 42; sustaining its inspiration, 0;

Condemning Christianity and the Church, 17; contending for them, 1;

7

Denying the Deity of Christ, 12; representing Him as the Son of God, 0."

People often wonder why the church is having a hard time today. The reason is evident. The godly father or mother (who brings to the birth and fosters youth to the point of young manhood and womanhood, to find all parental philosophies flung to the winds, and even parental care treated with contempt by the very children who splurge on the riches that represent father's sweat and mother's ceaseless endeavor), finds going difficult. So the Church of God, that brought education to the birth and cradled it into strength, is now treated with as much contempt by the schools that it created as was ever shown by degenerate offspring to devoted parents.

## EVOLUTION, WORLD-WIDE IN DEVASTATION

We come now to the consummation of the whole matter and to an understanding of the 94th Psalm.

*"How long shall the wicked triumph? How long shall they utter and speak hard things, and all the workers of iniquity boast themselves?*

*"They break in pieces thy people, O Lord, and afflict thine heritage.*

*"They slay the widow and the stranger, and murder the fatherless.*

*"Yet, they say, The Lord shall not see, neither shall the God of Jacob regard it.*

*"Understand, ye brutish among the people: and ye fools, when will ye be wise?"*

The very phraseology here suggests what we want to say:

*The doctrine of evolution is a brute-glorification.*

Old Thomas Carlyle was a keen thinker, and when on one occasion he gave the history of the Darwin family, he said, "I have known three generations of

8

them—grandfather, father and son" (He meant from Erasmus down to Charles). And he added, "Atheists all!" He told how he had found an old Erasmus Darwin seal, engraven with "OMNI EX CONCHIS" (everything from a clam shell). And then he added, "And this is what we have got to—all things from frog spawn—the GOSPEL OF DIRT!"

Yes, it's worse than a GOSPEL OF DIRT. It's a Gospel of *DESTRUCTION!*

Disraeli, in a speech at Oxford, once said, "The question before the world is this, 'Is man an ape or an angel?' I am on the side of the angels. I repudiate with indignation and abhorrence the contrary view."

Little wonder!

A few years ago *Our Baptist,* published in Chicago, had an article on "America Training Her Youth for the Lowest Brutality." It charged that one of the textbooks used in the College of the City of New York gave careful instruction on military training for breaking necks, gouging out eyes, knocking down and kicking into helplessness, and spoke of it as the art of sportsmanship. The book said "the object is to kill"; and explained "The principles of sportsmanship and consideration for your opponent have no place in the practical application of this work."

The volume added further, "This inherent desire to fight and to kill must be carefully watched for and encouraged."

Why not? If the doctrine of Darwin be true? Isn't that the law of life? Who blames the serpent for swallowing small fish, or even the big denizens of the sea for eating up the little ones?

Who blames the proud bird of the sky—the chief figure on our National Emblem, the eagle, for pouncing upon and making a meal of the dove?

Who blames the lion for quitting the jungle long enough to take out of the fold, the delicate morsel, a lamb?

9

If the theory of Darwin be true, these things belong to the laws of life; and if there be no personal God, Nature's laws can hardly be denominated wrong at any point. "Might makes right!" The strong should live; let the weak die! That's the Darwin doctrine!

Thomas Huxley, Darwin's associate in the philosophy, affirmed that evolution made of nature a "huge gladiatorial show" and "cockpit!" Strife and struggle constitute the essence of evolutionary process and the mainspring of progress.

*Such a philosophy is admirably adapted to Hitler objectives!*

In the *Minneapolis Star-Journal* Jan. 16, 1941, there was a two-column article on Hitler, in the course of which Hitler was reported by a former comrade and friend as having said, "In my great educative work, I am beginning with the young . . . With them I can make a new world. My teaching is hard. Weakness has to be knocked out of them. In my training schools a youth will grow up before which the world will shrink back. A violently active, dominating, intrepid, brutal youth—that is what I am after. It must be indifferent to pain. There must be no weakness or tenderness in it . . . In this way I shall eradicate the thousands of years of human domestication . . . I will tell you a secret. I have seen the vision of the new man—fearless and formidable. I shrank from him!"

Little wonder! He's the BEAST-MAN! But the amazing thing is that Hitler is not the originator of this idea. Any man or woman who will take the pains to read a book born of the war of 1914-18, and emanating from the pen of Dr. J. P. Bang, will discover that the German poets, philosophers, and preachers united their pens to propagate this same philosophy; and the Germany of today is not the Germany of twenty-five years ago, and still less that of fifty years ago when noble souls were quitting its soil for America's greater opportunities. That's why American Germans are seldom in sympathy with the war now being waged by their misguided relatives under Hitler leadership.

10

Emanuel Geibel, the poet-laureate of Germany, voiced the rising national egotism years ago by declaring that the world would yet be healed by Germanism, saying, "Some day it will happen, that the Lord will remove the shame of his people; He who spoke on the field of Leipzig, will speak once more in thunder. Then be of good cheer, O Germany. *This is the first sign!* When East and West unite to draw the sword against thee, then know that God will not forsake thee, if thou dost not forsake thyself. * * * Then let the chastening glow of a world-conflagration blaze forth, and do thou, the Imperial Eagle of the German land, arise like Phoenix from the flames!"

Take this from a German pastor also voicing himself in the time of the last World War, and it reveals how the misery of the world is the result of misguidance, for this pastor contorted the Lord's prayer into the following petition:

"Though the warrior's bread be scanty, do Thou work daily death and tenfold woe unto the enemy! Forgive in merciful long-suffering each bullet and each blow which misses its mark! Lead us not into the temptation of letting our wrath be too tame in carrying out Thy divine judgment! Deliver us and our Ally from the infernal Enemy and his servants on earth. Thine is the kingdom—the German land; may we, by aid of Thy steel-clad hand, achieve the power and the glory." Blasphemy!

Another sermon preached on one August 23 during the World War contains this statement:

"Germany is the future of humanity, a nation which is God's seed-corn for the future, the center of God's plans for the world," a sermon that wound up with the statement, "We love our earthly Fatherland so much that we gladly barter our heavenly for it."

Stanley High in May '41 *Reader's Digest* says of Hitler's Religion "God is Germany."

Hitler, then, bigoted as is his conceit, determined as are his murderous purposes, destructive as are his sub-

11

*215*

marines and bombs, pitiless as are his methods, is only the acme of a spirit which has grown in half a century into the bloody tyranny that stalks the world and gloats in evolution's philosophy—"MIGHT IS RIGHT; in the interest of the future, kill the weak, propagate the strong!"

*Finally, this philosophy, the pet of our American Universities, now threatens the life of the world.*

Fritz Philippi, another one of their poets, wrote what he called "World-Germany" during the last war and said, "Germany lies like a peaceful garden of God behind the wall of her armies." The poet hears the giant strides of the Germans armour-clad; the old era sinks into the ruin. *"But now the world shall have its coat cut according to German measure.* And as far as our swords flash and German blood flows, the circle of the earth shall come under the tutelage of German activity!" Think of Ernest Glauck's sacriligious statement, "Christ was great; but Hitler is greater."

While in the "Schlesische Zeitung" the following lines appeared:

"O God, do Thou accept us as strong and worthy to wield Thy fell sword of vengeance; as Thy faithful servants will we bleed and conquer for the right, and we will avenge the blood of our brethren with truly godlike courage. Oh, help us, Father, at the right time, Thou the Father of all justice!"

It's possible, then, for a people to become so enamored of brutal notions that Russian Bolshevik rulers can slay their own brethren in the flesh by the millions, and go to bed at night undisturbed by accusing consciences. And it is also possible for a Hitler to become so obsessed with the idea of being the chief warrior of the millenniums as to smite every weaker neighbor-nation. When asked the object and end of such revolution, he answered, "We do not know what the end will be, but we desire revolution." \* \* \* "I will compel the German people, who are hesitating before their destiny, to walk the road to greatness. I can attain my purpose only

12

through world revolution. We shall rejuvenate the world!"

Little wonder that Hermann Rauschining, Hitler's former party comrade, now a refugee in America, entitled his book and description of the German endeavor, "The Voice of Destruction."

In 1932, '33 and '34 he was a trusted official in the National Socialist party and president of the league of the Free City of Danzig. But when he finally became convinced that the movement, instead of being patriotic and progressive, was a nihilist revolution, threatening the world with ruin and Germany with the reputation of murder first and suicide later, he fled the fellowship and found safety on our soil. Little wonder that Hess also sickened and sought refuge in Scotland.

Professor Conklin of the University of Princeton said the human intellect reached the acme of its development two thousand years ago in Greece.

Hitler believes that the martial spirit has reached its acme in himself. He sums up the result—GERMANISM, and it's "a world on fire!"

We wonder what Charles Darwin would think of it, could he be permitted a resurrection today and the privilege of reviewing his philosophy's results.

But let it be understood that Charles Darwin didn't die without his fears for the future and his deep anxiety over the fruits of his own philosophy. Few of his followers will accept the testimony of dear LADY HOPE, his friend and neighbor, who went one day to his bedside for her accustomed visit, to find him sitting up in bed, wearing a soft embroidered dressing gown of rich purple shade. He was gazing out on the far-reaching stretch of woods and fields, and his face lit up as she entered the room. With a wave of his hand toward the scene, she noted that, in the other hand, he held an open Bible.

She asked, "What are you reading now?"

13

"HEBREWS," he answered. "I call it the Royal Book. Isn't it grand?"

She adds, "When I made some allusion to the strong opinions expressed by others on the history of Creation, its grandeur, and to the earlier chapters of the Book of Genesis, he seemed greatly distressed; his fingers twitched nervously, and a look of agony came over his face and he said:

" 'I was a young man, with unformed ideas! I threw out queries, suggestions, wondering all the time over everything; and to my astonishment the ideas took like wildfire. People made a religion of them.' "

Turning from his own theory, he spoke of the holiness of God and the grandeur of the Bible, and added, "I have a summer house in the garden, which holds about thirty people. I want you very much to speak there. I know you read the Bible in the villages. Tomorrow afternoon I should like the servants on the place, some tenants and a few of the neighbors to gather there. Will you speak to them?"

"What shall I speak about?" I asked.

He answered, "CHRIST JESUS, and His salvation! Is not that the best theme? And then I want you to sing some hymns with them. You lead on your small instrument, do you not? If you take the meeting at three o'clock this window will be open, and you will know that I am joining with you."

It was not long after that his soul took its flight. If it be true, as Lady Hope believed, that he deeply repented his philosophy and possibly accepted Jesus Christ as his Saviour, then only the statement of Scripture itself that in heaven *"there are no tears,"* could persuade me, that Charles Darwin was not bowed with an eternal grief over a philosophy that has baptized the world with blood.

## 44-88

### Great 60-Day Offer on Books

DR. W. B. RILEY has recently celebrated the 44th anniversary of his pastorate at Minneapolis and during this time he has published about 65 large volumes and collaborated with others in 10 additional. A dozen or more of these are now out of print. The following, however, can, for a limited time, be had at bargain prices:

*FORTY VOLUMES, THE BIBLE OF THE EXPOSITOR AND THE EVANGELIST.* Cloth-bound, goldlettered. Formerly $1.15 per volume; now 80c per volume, or $18.00, plus postage, for the entire set.

    COMMENTS: "It is worthy of a place beside Joseph Parker's 'People's Bible' and Alexander MacLaren's 'Expositions of Holy Scripture.'"—Dr. Paul W. Rood

    "The set is a benefit to my library and an inspiration to my heart."—Dr. A. C. Maxwell

    "I count this series of volumes valuable above everything in my library."—Dr. Luther Little

    "I am delighted with them. Seems almost too good to be true. Greatest set of books I ever owned."—Rev. William D. Gray

Formerly $1.50, all cloth-bound: (1) Revival Sermons, (2) Perennial Revival, (3) Pastoral Problems, (4) Is Jesus Coming Again? (5) The Dynamic of a Dream, Dr. Riley's biography.
*Now, any three to one order, $3.75; the five, $5.00*

Formerly $1.00, all cloth-bound: (1) Youth's Victory Lies This Way, (2) Wives of the Bible, (3) My Bible, An Apologetic, (4) Seven N. T. Soul-Winners, (5) Seven N. T. Converts, (6) The Conflict of Christianity With Its Counterfeits, (7) Re-Thinking the Church.
*Now, any three to one order, $2.50; the seven, $5.00.*

Paper-bound Booklets, 25c: (1) Saved or Lost, (2) The Victorious Life, (3) Wanted—A World Leader, (4) The Philosophies of Father Coughlin.
*Now, the four to one order, 75c.*

Formerly $1.75 for the three: (1) The Only Hope of Church or World (cloth), (2) The Blight of Unitarianism (paper), (3) The Conflict of Christianity With Its Counterfeits (paper).
NOW, THE THREE TO ONE ORDER, $1.25 . . . ORDER OF

**IRENE WOODS, 20 S. Eleventh St., Minneapolis, Minn.**

# ACKNOWLEDGMENTS

Riley, William Bell. *Are the Scriptures Scientific?* (1936): 1–32. Courtesy of Northwestern College, Berntsen Resource Center.

Riley, William Bell. *Darwinism; or, Is Man a Developed Monkey?* (1929): 3–24. Courtesy of Northwestern College, Berntsen Resource Center.

Riley, William Bell. *Darwin's Philosophy and the Flood.* (193?): 1–29. Courtesy of Northwestern College, Berntsen Resource Center.

Riley, William Bell. *Evolution—A False Philosophy.* (193?): 1–29. Courtesy of Northwestern College, Berntsen Resource Center.

Riley, William Bell. *The Scientific Accuracy of the Sacred Scriptures.* (1920): 1–20. Courtesy of Northwestern College, Berntsen Resource Center.

Riley, William Bell. *The Theory of Evolution Tested by Mathematics.* (193?): 1–28. Courtesy of Northwestern College, Berntsen Resource Center.

Riley, William Bell. *The Theory of Evolution—Does It Tend to Atheism?* (192?): 1–19. Courtesy of Northwestern College, Berntsen Resource Center.

Riley, William Bell . *The Theory of Evolution—Does It Tend To Anarchy?* (192?): 1–16. Courtesy of Northwestern College, Berntsen Resource Center.

Riley, William Bell. *Hitlerism; or, The Philosophy of Evolution in Action.* (1941): 1–14. Courtesy of Northwestern College, Berntsen Resource Center.

For Product Safety Concerns and Information please contact our EU
representative  GPSR@taylorandfrancis.com
Taylor & Francis Verlag GmbH, Kaufingerstraße 24, 80331 München, Germany

www.ingramcontent.com/pod-product-compliance
Lightning Source LLC
Chambersburg PA
CBHW062141300426
44115CB00012BA/1993